FUTUREPROOF

7 KEY PILLARS FOR DIGITAL TRANSFORMATION SUCCESS

DANIEL NEWMAN WITH OLIVIER BLANCHARD

FUTUREPROOF

Daniel Newman with Olivier Blanchard

ISBN 978-0-692-94724-1

First Printing 2017

Publisher: Broadsuite, Inc.
T: 817-480-3038
www.broadsuite.com

TABLE OF CONTENTS

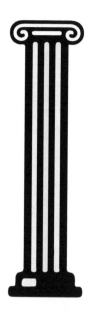

INTRODUCTION:

In *Building Dragons* we introduced you to the new paradigms of the *Experience Economy* and outlined how new technologies are disrupting the world of business and reinventing it for the digital age: Cloud, mobile, Big Data, mixed reality, the Internet of Things... an avalanche of transformative new technologies and capabilities have steadily displaced the Fortune 500's old guard, shifted market value toward smart new companies like Amazon, Facebook and Google, and allowed already successful tech companies like Apple, Qualcomm, Samsung, and IBM to expand their reach and broaden their market horizons. We brought purpose and structure to *Digital Transformation*, and made the case for a new kind of highly adaptive and innovative business model that combines the can-do, agile, entrepreneurial spirit of tech startups and the experience, stability and market power of established, incumbent companies.

Rather than spend nearly 200 pages extolling the virtues of unicorns—young companies valued at $1B or more—we focused our attention on ways to create a more viable approach to technology integration and market leadership—building dragons, or companies that enjoy the best of both worlds, that combine the best of the new and the old. We challenged business leaders to rebuild their own companies and prepare them for what the business world of 2025, 2030 and beyond will demand of them.

We've since had a lot of conversations with business executives about this. We've listened to their concerns, challenges and questions like: *What technologies should we invest in? What ratio of public and private cloud is ideal? How will we overcome resistance to change? How will we convince our board that changing our business model this far ahead of our competitors is worth the risk? How will we learn to become a technologically-savvy company when none of our senior executives are technologically savvy?* But no question resonated more with us than: *What company should we become?*

It seems an odd question at first. The reflex is to simply say *"more like a dragon"* or *"the same company that you are now, only more digital and technologically driven,"* but that's incorrect.

What company should we become?

If Apple had asked that question in 2002, the easy answer probably would have been *"a better computer company."* That answer would have been wrong too. The future of business won't look like the last 10 years. If you own a business today, that business will either radically change in the next decade, or it will fade and die. IBM isn't the same company it was a decade ago. Nike isn't the same company it was a decade ago. Ford, GE, Amazon and Google are not the same companies they were a decade ago. Apple is making phones and watches now. IBM transitioned from hardware to the Cloud, and is making enormous progress in the field of artificial intelligence and cognitive computing. Amazon still sells books, but it also sells everything else now, competes against Netflix, has managed to make everyone want voice-activated smart speakers, and wants to send people into space. Google is making gorgeous smartphones, outstanding laptops and even getting into the smart home market. Whatever business you happen to be in today doesn't matter. Your business model in 10 years will not be what it is today. You will have a different company.

What company should we become? The question resonates. It also demands an answer.

This question is why we decided to call our book *Futureproof.* We wanted to give you a framework, a methodology and tools with which to transform any organization into the sort of company where change and disruption often turns into opportunities and success. To that end, we looked at what made highly adaptive companies different from the rest of the field, companies like Nike, Ford, Apple, Microsoft, Amazon, and GE, to name a few. We looked at their behaviors and traits. We studied how they made decisions and how they managed to make many of the right bets when other companies didn't. We wanted to know what made them different, what made them better at rolling with punches and evolving with the times.

What we found is that all of these companies, whether they realize it or not, focus on seven fundamental pillars that, when combined, create precisely the right mix of mindset, capabilities and competencies that allow them to adapt better, innovate faster and turn change into a strategic advantage. These seven pillars—or areas of focus, if you prefer—are: *experiences, people, change, innovation, leadership, technology,* and *culture.* Without fail, every company we studied that demonstrated an ability to make itself future-proof invested in, prioritized and nurtured these seven aspects of its business. We intend to make sense of all seven of them here.

To keep things simple, we have structured *Futureproof* into seven chapters, one for each of the seven pillars, and filled its pages with as many insights, case studies and real-world examples as we could fit into each chapter. *Futureproof* is by no means a complete collection of futureproofing examples. For every anecdote and data point we included in the book, a dozen ended up on the "next time" pile. We hope that the ones we selected are the most useful to you.

CHAPTER 1:

EXPERIENCES

How Experiences, Not Products or Services, are Becoming the New Battleground for 21st Century Businesses.

SHIFTING GEARS: RETOOLING FOR THE EXPERIENCE ECONOMY

While "the experience economy" may be a relatively new concept, good business always has been about creating consistently remarkable experiences. Think about it. What ultimately makes a restaurant successful? A hotel? A car manufacturer? A musical artist? A sports team? A retailer? When have consistently positive, remarkable, delightful experiences not been at the heart of every successful business? Conversely, when have consistently disappointing, subpar, or horrible experiences not harmed and even killed businesses?

One could argue that the current shift to an experience economy isn't so much a business shift as it is a shift in our collective awareness regarding what makes businesses successful.

IF EXPERIENCES ARE ABOUT EMOTION, BUSINESS SUCCESS IS DRIVEN MOSTLY BY EMOTION.

Love and hate, desire and apathy, buying and not buying, are all binary choices.

Some decisions are naturally more rational, logical and data-based than others. Business decisions, more often than not, should be pragmatic rather than emotional. For example, what companies to partner with, what technologies to invest in, what markets to go after, how much to spend on R&D projects and marketing, or how many resources to apply to solving this problem instead of that. In a similar vein, some types of consumer decisions tend to be more pragmatic than others. For example, what stocks to invest in, how much money to contribute to a 401K, what kind of health insurance package to sign up for, how much to spend on replacement tires, or whether to buy the generic brand or the premium brand. But even these decisions are driven, at least in part, by emotion. Risk versus reward, for instance, will impact which stocks you might want to invest in. Fear may influence decisions relating to 401K contributions and health insurance purchases. Preferences and personal bias toward or against a brand may influence a tire purchase. Few decisions, even those which we consider to be logical, fact-based and pragmatic, are ever immune from emotion.

When it comes to the vast majority of consumer decisions, emotion, not cold, logical, pragmatic calculations, influence purchases. Emotional responses to advertising, for instance, are two to three times more likely to influence purchase intent than the information contained in the ad.[1] Consumer perceptions of brand-associated value, product price points, design narratives, crowd desirability, cultural status, and more tend to drive purchase behaviors. Why do some people drive five extra miles to buy their coffee at Starbucks? Why do some people spend twice as much for a MacBook than for an HP or Microsoft laptop with roughly equivalent specs? Why do some people shop at Target but not at Walmart? Why do some people prefer Ford to GM, or Frosted Flakes to Raisin Bran or Levi's to Wrangler?

---

[1]Damasio, Antonio. Descartes' Error. Penguin Books, 2005.

We all make thousands of decisions all day long, most of them subconsciously. The process of making choices about what to wear, what to eat, what songs to listen to, when to take a sip of water, when to reply to an email, whether to smile or just nod, and purchasing decisions aren't all that different. While it may take some time to justify and actually decide to make a purchase, purchase intent, like most other decisions, happens subconsciously and quickly. In that sense, it isn't so different from our built-in fight or flight response. It's about want or don't want, or trust or don't trust. These are the same types of binary decisions we subconsciously, one might say automatically, make all day, and most of these are driven by emotion.

And what helps shape our emotions? Experience.

Bees sting. Being stung hurts. Experience tells us not to play with bees.

Strawberries are delicious. You used to love strawberries as a child. Experience makes you crave strawberries when you smell fresh ones at the store or market.

Rental car company A almost made you miss your plane last time you used them. They were rude and overcharged you the time before that. You don't like to use that rental car company anymore and won't unless you absolutely have to. Rental car company B, on the other hand, always has immaculate cars, their mobile app is super easy to use and they have great customer service. Rental car company B is now your rental car company of choice.

Your last experience at a Disney theme park was so amazing that you can't wait to share it with your other set of grandkids, and you have recommended it to all of your neighbors and colleagues for months.

Let's face it, emotions fuel experiences. These experiences in build expectations and biases about people, places, products, and companies. At their core, emotions and experiences are either good or bad, positive or negative. The subconscious binary calculus that we base thousands of decisions every day is an integral part of our internal catalog of decision parameters. Brand A: Good. Brand B: Bad. Brand A: Amazing. Brand B: Horrible.

Experiences matter, whether you own a car rental company, a restaurant chain, a hardware store, a hotel, a consumer electronics company, a coffee shop, a moving company, an airline, or you are an Airbnb host, a landscaper, an accountant, a dentist, a yoga instructor, a movie director, an accountant, or a corporate recruiter, Experiences are everything. It only takes one-tenth of a second to form a first impression about a person and 50 milliseconds to form a first impression about a website. More importantly, it takes only one negative interaction with an employee or automated process to lose a potential customer forever. If that negative interaction is more than just marginally negative, if it escalates into an argument, or an altercation, or an egregious breach of customer service or expectations of quality, it takes only a few seconds for it to be uploaded to social networks where it may be shared by tens of thousands, even millions of people.

Love and delight build successful brands. Hate and disappointment destroys them. Whether you're representing Apple, BMW, Coca Cola, HBO, Amazon, Oakley, Regal Cinemas, Verizon, or United Airlines, one hundred percent of that emotional spectrum is driven by experiences.

DOES THE COMPANY THAT CONSISTENTLY CREATES THE BEST EXPERIENCES WIN?

Leaders in remarkable customer experiences aren't hard to find. They are the companies that manage to delight and impress customers consistently. These are companies like Disney, Apple, and Tesla. Even in small, hyperlocal markets, delightful, impressive companies generally are well known. For example, the special coffee shop you can't get enough of, the best dry cleaner in town, the authentic pizzeria in the renovated old cotton mill by the river, the best massage therapist in the country who just happens to work in your area code, the most talented tax attorney you've ever met, or the wedding photographer your friends can't stop raving about. If you really stop to take inventory of companies that understand how to consistently create the best experiences for their customers, you will realize that, while most companies fall short, companies that don't are in no short supply. Execution is the hard part, but tens of thousands of businesses around the world are onto this, and they are delivering something unique, special and valuable to their customers, which makes them successful year after year after year.

The trick is not only to create remarkable experiences, but to do so consistently. It isn't enough to have really good days here and there, or really good interactions with customers on a regular basis. To be truly successful at the experience game, you have to create remarkable experiences 100 percent of the time. That doesn't happen by accident. It isn't the result of an afterthought. Getting it right 100 percent of the time (or as near to 100 percent as you can realistically get), requires commitment, focus, discipline, and painstaking patience. Consistency is the most important ingredient in the overall experience design formula. Consistency is what puts companies like Starbucks, Apple, Tesla, Ray Ban, Coca Cola, Nespresso, Wyndham Hotels, and even Amazon at the top of so many people's lists when the time comes to make a purchase, take a break or just get away.

Let's face it, Amazon doesn't create the world's most extraordinary online shopping experiences. Even if you love Starbucks, their baristas don't come close to making the best latte you'll ever drink. One could argue successfully that Jaguar, BMW, Lexus, and Land Rover design cooler shopping experiences than Tesla. The unpacking of an iMac doesn't necessarily blow away the unpacking of a Microsoft Surface Studio either. The best experiences don't always win and can't always scale. Creating "the best" experience isn't always the goal, but, more often than not, creating the *right* experience does. In some cases, nostalgia wins. For example, when someone says, "The smell of this breakfast cereal reminds me of my childhood." In some cases, surprising experiences win, like when someone thinks: "I hadn't expected that… but I like it. That was clever." Sometimes, consistency and reliability win, like when someone thinks: "I never have to worry about something going wrong. No matter where I am or what I order, there's never a problem."

Companies like Disney, Apple and Tesla tend to blend as many of these dimensions of experience as possible. They are true experience companies. They obsess about every minute detail of the customer experience, and it shows. Every step of their customer experience journey is carefully studied, mapped, considered, measured, optimized, improved, and, on a regular basis, reinvented.

Companies like Google, Facebook and Amazon aren't necessarily as focused on creating the best possible customer experiences, but they prioritize which experiences they feel are most important to their business and focus on those. For Google, those experiences are mostly speed (searches have to feel instantaneous), accuracy (from search results to ad targeting, there is no room for being off target), and ease of use (Google's home page is as simple and user-friendly as it gets). For Facebook, those experiences start with the newsfeed. What do users want to see in it? What kinds of content? What kinds of news? Facebook obsesses about getting this right and uses some of the world's most complex algorithms to deliver ever-more relevant newsfeeds that, in theory, should feel like they were custom curated for each individual user. As busy and layered as Facebook's design is (especially compared to Google's), Facebook also obsesses about trying to make every feature (from liking, commenting on and sharing content to adjusting account settings, browsing groups or searching for specific items) easy to find and adjust. Amazon, like Facebook, obsesses about making the content and products users are most likely to be interested in find them. Instead of news items, Amazon's algorithms deliver ever more relevant suggestions, based on previous searches, product and content affinities, and hundreds of other behavioral data points. If Amazon can't find what users want before they even know that they want it, or if the algorithms aren't quite tuned in to some users' needs and timing, Amazon makes searching for that one special something as easy as Google. To a great extent, that is the idea behind voice-activated speakers and natural language processing. Amazon Echo makes search as simple as speech. Users don't have to sit at their computers and pull up Amazon on their browsers. They don't have to wake up their phones and swipe through an apps. All they have to do is say what they want, and Amazon delivers.

The power to craft the right kinds of experiences and deliver on their promises isn't difficult to see. All of these companies started from nothing. What makes them so successful isn't where they started or when they started doing things right. It's what they do *now* that matters. It's what they choose to focus on and be known for that makes the difference between being category leaders with massive market share and being also-in industry players with single-digit market share.

You don't have to be a billion dollar company to accomplish this. Small and mid-sized businesses pull this off on a daily basis. Greenville, South Carolina-based Methodical Coffee, for instance, is a small coffee shop that sits in a glass and concrete corner of the growing southern city's hip refurbished downtown. The raw floors remind customers that the shop probably sits where an old cotton mill once did, conveying a sense of authenticity to visitors as soon as they walk in. The foundations of the shop are literally tied to at least a century of local history. The walls are white, the wood and metal décor purposely minimalist, the ceilings high and airy. The record player behind the counter is a throwback to an era that Millennial visitors venerate its analog mystique, and that makes Xers and Boomers feel familiar and welcoming. The smell of coffee is thick and inviting. A glass display advertises authentic-looking local artisan baked goods like chocolate croissants alongside innovative patisseries that beg conversation and explanation. The baristas are everything baristas should be—friendly, edgy, welcoming, and supremely well trained in the dark arts of coffee making. The menu on the wall is minimalist and only shows a fraction of what you can order there. The cash registers are slick touchscreens set on swivels. Ordering and paying are a breeze. The entire onboarding experience leaves out-of-town visitors delighted, impressed and surprised. You can watch these visitors turn to each other with impressed looks and comment, before they've even tasted their drinks, that they wish they had a coffee shop "like this" back home. Most patrons watch the baristas prepare their orders. Whether they asked for a pour-over or something requiring a shot of espresso, the performance continues. The equipment the baristas use is gorgeous, designed as much for form as for function. Every gesture is the result of hundreds, if not thousands of hours of repetition, and designed to create the perfect coffee drink every single time. It is the coffee shop's equivalent of a traditional Japanese tea ceremony, only this one is fast, matter-of-fact and stripped bare of protocol. Patrons watch, somewhere between mesmerized and entertained, as unknown barista technologies and the fluent manifestation of their expertise evoke notions of alchemy. When the coffee comes, even the receptacle it's served in bears the unique brand of the experience. Espresso drinks are served in gorgeous Willow-patterned china one would not expect to fit in so well there. The napkins are high thread count cotton and look hand finished. Everything is luxury pretending to be common. Then you take your first sip, and you discover that

Methodical's coffee tastes unlike any coffee you've ever tasted, delicious to even the most discriminant coffee connoisseur.

If a small coffee shop in South Carolina can pull this off, and thousands of businesses around the world, from hole-in-the-wall diners and mom-and-pop bakeries to boutique hotels and specialty sporting goods stores. Truth is, any company can pull off what Methodical Coffee has done. It doesn't matter if you own a dental practice, an auto repair shop, a law firm, an engineering services firm, an IT consultancy, or a bank, if you focus on creating the right kinds of experiences for your customers, you will stand out. You will give everyone who discovers your business a reason to come back and tell everyone they know how special you are.

Customer and user experiences are what ultimately make companies like BMW, Apple, Amazon, and Facebook successful. Those experiences are what makes them unique and more relevant than their competitors.

Being different and special isn't taking a risk. Being like everyone else is the risk. Not crafting unique and relevant experiences is the risk. When you want to stand out, when you *need* to stand out, blowing off experience design and allowing your business to be indistinguishable from the herd is where the risk really lies.

Customer experience design cannot be an afterthought. It has to be treated as a business priority. Whether companies ever get to a place where they appoint a chief customer experience design officer, partner with customer experience design firms or create thorough experience design guidelines for themselves is a matter of choice. What matters is that they take this seriously and make experience design one of their primary points of focus.

ECOSYSTEMS OF EXPERIENCE: ADDING LAYERS AND SCALE

Most established businesses can't just turn on a dime. If experience design wasn't a priority until now, it is unrealistic to expect them to suddenly become experience-driven companies. Change comes in steps. Steps lead to milestones. Change happens over time. The first steps are always the hardest, but they don't have to be the biggest.

We're big fans of pilot programs, low cost, low risk, small scale programs to test an idea or a theory. It's a "let's try this and see what happens" approach like adding a few more plants in the front office, hooking up some flat screen displays on the walls of your waiting room, injecting the air with a hint of pleasant smells, softening the light inside the building, adding texture to walls and partitions, modifying the acoustic qualities of an open workspace, replacing the table and swivel chairs in the conference room with armchairs and a coffee table, or moving the office to a building with more raw brick, wooden floors and natural light.

Companies don't have to start with big experience changes. They don't have to reinvent the wheel overnight. They can start with small improvements here and there and see what happens. You wouldn't believe the impact one small positive change can make. We've seen companies start to turn employee morale around just by making a few slight adjustments to their workday experiences, from revamping the break room to be less austere to introducing better collaboration software. Introducing couches in hallways, where people can get away from their desks and have a quick conversation about a project with a colleague can do wonders to improve innovation and problem-solving at a company. Introducing an appointment management and FAQ app for your patients can turn your previously anemic medical practice into a local success story.

This isn't mere incrementalism, by the way. It's change, one step at a time. It's experience design experimentation, one experiment at a time. It's continuous improvement in manageable, measurable, self-validating steps. Before long, those small changes start to add up to something big. The better things get, the easier it is to try the next idea and build on previous successes. The model is different for every company. There aren't any universal best practices. The way Nike does this is not the way Air France does it, but the principles are always the same. You don't have to rebrand. You don't need a complete makeover. Avoid the one-size-fits-all solution or the big bang marketing coup. Do this one step at a time, one degree of customer or employee experience at a time. Measure your success in improved morale, a visible increase in smiles, or a steady uptick in positive mentions and visitor traffic. Walk around your stores and offices, and feel if there's a positive difference.

If you're a business leader, don't just rely on numbers and metrics. Walk the floor, visit locations and watch people. See for yourself what works and what doesn't. Experiences are about emotion, right? Go out there and feel the change. Go find out if it's working or not. Go see if something needs more work. Talk to customers and employees, and listen to what they have to say. If a small coffee shop in South Carolina can figure this out, companies as large as Apple can do it year after year, and even banks like Ally and Ubank reinvent customer experiences for banking (in their case, using a mobile-first approach), any company can do it.

For Ally, one of the key catalysts in the transformation of customer experience was the company's CIO, Michael Baresich. Here's what he did:

- Since customer experiences were going to rely so much on technology effectiveness, he focused on prioritizing IT's role in the design and implementation process.

- Because IT needed to focus on solving problems and on innovation rather than on merely keeping its existing infrastructure going, he focused on making IT more efficient.

- Because improving IT efficiency meant unburdening IT, he began by tasking IT with eliminating old and burdensome technologies, and cutting unnecessary costs.

- Speaking of cost, Baresich understood that change of that magnitude, even if it didn't all happen at once, required a high degree of accountability. That early in the process, the sort of accountability he was looking for was financial. He had to be able to convey cost-benefit equations to his board accurately and effectively. This meant that IT leaders would have to start thinking more like investors and entrepreneurs than mere managers. Ergo: New skillsets, more accountability, more empowerment, and asking managers to start behaving like leaders.

- He tripled down on data security, without which none of what Ally did in terms of customer experiences would ultimately matter.

- By injecting more leadership and entrepreneurial behaviors into his IT ecosystem, and clearly articulating his vision, Baresich drove that ecosystem toward an innovation-focused, mission-driven mindset he could apply easily to customer experience design.

- The working group also was not limited to IT. Ally isn't burdened by silos, so Baresich made sure collaboration and insights moved freely across the organization. Informal working groups were created to participate in discussions. Whiteboarding was common during the ideation process and continued to play a role in subsequent discussions.

- Ally also separated the moving parts of this project into distinct categories: What to build, what to buy or license, what to find partners for, and so on. There was no reason to do everything in-house. The trick to making such a complex endeavor manageable was to decide what parts of it needed to be custom built, and what parts could be brought in and integrated.

There are dozens of lessons here, from the need to jettison burdensome technologies, processes and behaviors to empowering managers to become leaders, but the one that strikes us the most is how much of the process didn't immediately address customer experience design. The end goal was to create a completely new type of banking experience for consumers, but the work that went into building it was almost entirely focused on digital transformation and futureproofing the company's IT department before the design of those experiences could be delivered to the market. Incorporating Touch ID, Apple Pay, Voice Assist, and chatbots into the overall banking experience came later.

We still think of Ally as a bank, but it isn't just a bank anymore. It transformed itself into a technology company that happens to be a bank. Its IT department doesn't look or operate like a traditional IT department. IT now drives, enables and optimizes every aspect of Ally's business. It also functions as a funnel for new technologies, new capabilities and transformative innovation. That's a different model from the one most people think about when they envision a bank. This, combined with a data-driven, flat, collaborative, empowering, experience-focused company culture, makes Ally as futureproof as a bank can get. But it doesn't stop there. Ally also makes a habit of sending scouts to Silicon Valley to shop for new technologies, gauge where consumer and technology markets may be going, and see what venture capitalists are investing in. These scouts aren't just IT professionals. They come from all corners of the company and represent dozens of disciplines. In other words, Ally is not operating inside its own corporate bubble or even inside its industry bubble. It doesn't care to conform to the norms of competitors that still operate as if the world were changing more slowly than it is. We cannot stress how crucial this is.

1. Any company today that is not firmly plugged into the tech innovation space is not going to be able to compete against companies that are.

2. Any company that doesn't get out of its own bubble is not going to be able to pull off an effective digital transformation, let alone find itself in a position to design uniquely amazing experiences for its customers.

3. Any company that doesn't approach items 1 and 2 as multi-discipline efforts that involve every department is not going to be effective either. You can't have half of your departments rowing in one direction, and the rest confused about where you are rowing to and why.

One final point, focused on Item 2: companies that operate in industries known for lousy customer experiences are never going to be able to escape the vicious cycle of poor customer experience if they don't leave the safety of their industry bubbles and go look for inspiration elsewhere.

Airlines and utility companies are a perfect example of this. If airlines really want to start delivering better customer experiences for economy travelers, they need to look at how other service industries create great customer experiences without charging a premium. Technology is just one aspect of this. Sending executives and employees to Silicon Valley isn't going to be enough. They also need to learn from hoteliers, restaurateurs, spa operators, retailers, interior designers, psychologists, school teachers, yoga instructors, and artists. The more different your inspiration is from your industry, the better. Innovation is always driven by inspiration, and inspiration comes from being exposed to new ideas and different points of view. Innovation, including experience-focused innovation, requires leaving the bubble and going out into the world to see how other people and companies do what they do.

This sort of thinking is how the future of the experience economy is being built and how experience design, as a matter of operational focus, helps drive digital transformation and the futureproofing of companies, regardless of industry.

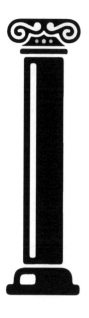

CHAPTER 2:

PEOPLE

Automation or Not, People Are Still the Holy Grail of Business

We mentioned earlier in the book how GE's digital-first approach to futureproofing focused heavily on establishing a culture of competence, ownership and accountability at the senior leadership level. As expected, that culture trickled down into every layer of the organization, and spread far and wide, inserting itself in every operational touchpoint. Jim Fowler, GE's CIO during Jeff Immelt's tenure as CEO, shared that he hadn't hired anyone from any of the top schools in the last five years who didn't know how to code. Fowler also acknowledged something we advocate throughout this book, but rarely hear Fortune 500 executives express as clearly and succinctly as he does: A transition to "digital" requires that hires adapt to entirely new work requirements.

Digital transforms companies, and, when it does, it transforms the way everyone works at these companies. It seems like an obvious thing to say, a no-brainer insight, but it isn't.

What Fowler referenced isn't just a model in which workers develop new skills, then go on working the way they used to with a few more additional capabilities. He is conveying that, when a company digitally transforms, everything changes. When companies as successful and innovative as GE start asking business grads and newly-minted engineers from the world's top schools if they can code, take that as a hint that things are changing in a big way.

THE MILLENNIAL EFFECT

By 2020, millennials will comprise nearly half of the global workforce. This is the single trend, data point or insight that can help us understand the fundamental shift transforming the workplace and collaboration tools.

Millennials enjoy a practical understanding of efficient workflows that is vastly different from those endured by many of their predecessors. This is the result of millennials being largely unburdened by the limitations of productivity and collaboration tools of bygone eras, and because they have spent the last decade developing naturally collaborative skills and processes by way of apps, mobile devices and social medias. As a result, millennials bring their own technology requirements, their own expectations, and their own way of doing things to today's workplace.

Collaboration via email, which always was limited and fraught with inefficiencies, has been bypassed by faster, slicker and less interruptive messaging apps. Physical meetings largely have been replaced by video. Cumbersome desktops, calendars and handsets have been replaced by laptops and smartphones. Like it or not, millennials already are reshaping the workplace to fit their own collaborative styles. Empowered by new technologies like mobile devices, the cloud and a rich ecosystem of apps, they are bypassing operational and technological bottlenecks that the majority of their less technologically savvy peers still wrestle with.

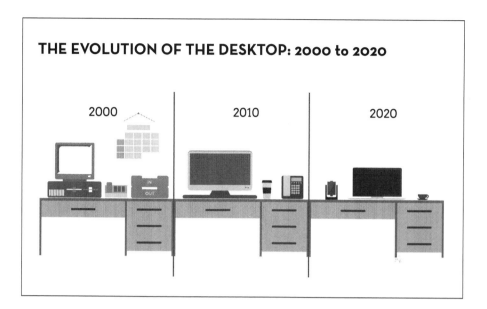

THE EVOLUTION OF THE DESKTOP: 2000 to 2020

2000   2010   2020

As more millennials populate and take over IT departments and other key line of business roles, the tendency to replace aging, cumbersome and increasingly ineffective "enterprise" collaboration tools with a new generation of agile, cloud-based collaboration apps is taking hold and spreading fast. Much of the digital transformation reshaping the world of business is driven by millennial decision makers letting go of outdated technologies, methodologies and mindsets, and replacing them with something better and far more efficient. Today's most innovative companies increasingly are led and managed by digitally-literate millennials, a trend that is unlikely to change in the next five to 10 years.

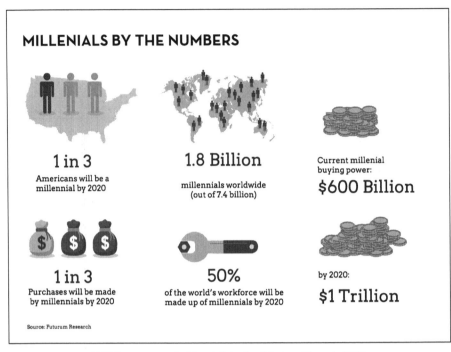

MILLENIALS BY THE NUMBERS

1 in 3
Americans will be a
millennial by 2020

1.8 Billion
millennials worldwide
(out of 7.4 billion)

Current millenial
buying power:
$600 Billion

1 in 3
Purchases will be made
by millennials by 2020

50%
of the world's workforce will be
made up of millennials by 2020

by 2020:
$1 Trillion

Source: Futurum Research

50%: Percentage of millennials in the global workforce in 2020.

It also is worth noting that by 2020, one in three Americans will be a millennial, making one in three purchases. Businesses need to align themselves to the technology expectations of millennials in their extended markets. That alignment begins within, with the adoption of consumer-friendly digital technologies and a mindset predicated on operational agility, velocity of execution and continuous business innovation at scale.

THE DIGITAL NATIVE EFFECT

Digital natives, not just millennials, are fundamentally transforming the workplace.

Take the evolution of the work desk, for instance. It's as simple and visible symptom of this change as any. Ten years ago, the white-collar workspace would have consisted of a desktop PC, a hard-wired phone, a physical calculator, a printed calendar of some kind, inbox and outbox trays, drawers of paper files slipped into actual folders, and maybe even a fax machine.

Fast forward to today and that same workspace, assuming the company isn't lagging dangerously behind, is likely to look much simpler, with little more than a laptop, a smartphone, a few pocket-sized dongles and mobile accessories, and a charging pad.

The change is partly because most of yesterday's physical business tools were replaced by less cumbersome ones. There's no need for typewriters anymore. Space is at a premium and data storage is cheap, so companies eliminated paper files and filing cabinets. Email has replaced faxes. These changes are a matter of economics and operational efficiency.

These changes are also partly because work is increasingly mobile. You can't take a typewriter or a fax machine home with you, or on a trip, but you can take your laptop. Productivity apps live on phones too. Cloud-based solutions enable workers to do their work from virtually anywhere as long as they have minimal connectivity and enough power to run their devices.

A third reason for the changes is that the workforce itself is changing. Xers and early millennials, who adopted digital technologies at work and experienced the transition from analog workspaces to digital ones, are being joined by a generation of digital natives who have never worked in analog environments. These digital native workers have only known email, messaging apps, mobile collaboration tools, and digital productivity. Companies that don't operate on the same technological planet as these new young professionals cannot possibly hope to attract them, let alone compete against companies that do. Because the nature of the workforce itself is changing, the nature of work itself is changing. It *has* to.

ATTITUDES TOWARD WORK ALSO ARE CHANGING

Another aspect of the changes affecting the way we work is illustrated by the evolution of attitudes and behaviors toward work, particularly now that productivity and collaboration tools are so mobile.

Let's start with a simple, powerful data point. According to the 2017 *Breaking Barriers 2020: How CIOs are Shaping the Future of Work* report by Fuze[2], 85 percent of workers surveyed found the idea of working from home appealing. This number is remarkable given the potential social and professional benefits of working face-to-face with people and the rewarding nature of an engaging workplace. Regardless of technological advances, the data suggest that a large proportion of workplaces fail to motivate and engage employees, and/or provide them with a rewarding work environment. Although this calls for a separate discussion about workplace cultures and experience design, we note that unappealing or otherwise demotivating workplaces may contribute to the adoption of productivity tools whose purpose is essentially to allow workers to *escape* to work environments they find more rewarding. Another reason may also be the push toward achieving a work-life balance, especially in households where having some work attendance flexibility would go a long way toward, for instance, picking up children from school or being there when they are home. It also addresses many employees' medical needs, helps work around educational requirements for student workers and can, in many cases, help workers who prefer to work without interruptions improve their productivity.

The response was not as positive when the same workers were asked more directly if they wanted to work from home. Instead of 85 percent positive replies, responses dropped to 71 percent or below with rather clear generational differences.

Digital natives, millennials and Xers (that is, everyone under the age of 45) answered along a relatively similar trajectory, with most answering yes. But, when 45 to 54- year olds and those 55 and older were asked if they would like to work from home, only half responded in the affirmative.

---

[2]Breaking Barriers 2020: How CIOs Are Shaping the Future of Work. Fuze, 2017.

To be fair, it is difficult to gauge whether younger workers are more open to working from home because they are more comfortable with digital productivity and collaboration tools, because they don't feel being at the office is particularly useful, or because of varying attitudes about needing to be in a physical office to do their job versus getting the job done regardless of location.

There appears to be a correlation between attitudes toward where work should be done, and the adoption of mobile productivity and collaboration tools (and methodologies). The more likely an age group is to favor working from home, the more likely that same age group is to use mobile productivity and collaboration tools, and vice versa.

THE COMMODITIZATION OF WORK VS REINVENTING THE ORG CHART

We probably could dedicate an entire book to the commoditization of work, but, for the sake of expediency, let's just break down its main threads into digestible insights that are most relevant to futureproofing:

- Work is becoming more mobile.

- Work is becoming more flexible.

- Smart automation (bots, AIs, digital assistants) is increasingly injecting itself into daily human tasks and functions.

- Contract work and the "gig economy" continue to gain favor with independent professionals and COOs alike. These types of work also are increasingly supported by a user-friendly technology infrastructure that makes it easy and relatively frictionless for talent and businesses to come together on a limited and contractual basis. These business-contractor relationships can be recurring or not, short or long term, and essentially amount to a vast ecosystem of specialized on-demand workers who can come and go based on an organization's needs.

Uber and Lyft are among the most visible examples of companies that have successfully leveraged technology to put specialized contractors (in these cases, drivers) at the core of their business models, but they are far from the only ones. Marketing and advertising agencies routinely work with outside contractors when projects and their funding demand an influx of specialized manpower. Thus, graphic designers, copywriters, developers, voice actors, animators, social media strategists, and so on get brought onboard for the duration of a project.

Countless organizations also leverage outside talent to fix security problems, build software, revamp websites, clean up databases, train their workforce, and so on. While companies once prided themselves on the size of their workforce, boasting hundreds, thousands, or sometimes tens of thousands of employees as a sign of success and growth, companies now increasingly turn to a more hybrid model of core capacity (employees) and flexible capacity (contractors and part-time employees).

The increasingly mobile nature of work, from productivity to collaboration, makes this hybrid model all the more attractive and effective. Bringing contractors and project teams together even 10 years ago would have posed tremendous challenges and inefficiencies. Communication and collaboration tools like email and conference calls were not ideal for agile collaboration. Different working styles and hidden commitments to other projects could severely alter deliverables and project schedules. Accountability was an issue as well. Today, one-touch video conferencing allows project teams to meet anywhere, anytime. All they need is an app like Cisco Spark on their devices, and they can connect face-to-face to discuss ideas or solve a problem. Business messaging apps are far more natural and time management friendly than email, as conversations are more fluid and linear, and the medium lends itself to short exchanges rather than manifestos and tirades that email discussions often turn into. The portability of these discussions, and searchability of keywords and timelines, also makes project management more fluid and effective, reducing the need for project teams to physically meet in one place or to work around everyone's schedules.

Task automation is another aspect of the commoditization of work, as we mentioned in our bullets above. There is a much larger discussion to be had about the future of work as automation increasingly takes over certain job functions. That discussion should be far more about human/machine partnerships than human vs machines and the end of employment as we know it. It is a discussion we intend to dive into soon, so stay tuned. For now, what we want to point out that, as digital assistants, bots and AIs begin to take on our menial, repetitive, time-sucking tasks, we are able to focus on tasks that matter. Automation doesn't have to take away your job. Automation can just as easily make you better at your job, including being more productive and effective. This is true whether you are a CEO, a middle manager or the most junior hire in your organization.

We sense a lot of fear and uncertainty about automation when we talk with decision makers and their staffs. Will I be replaced by an algorithm? Will I be replaced by a robot or an AI? The easiest answer is *maybe*, but that doesn't have to be the case. What may happen instead is that your job will be enhanced by bots and AIs. Maybe you will manage a team of digital assistants and bots, who will in turn help manage you. This collaboration between humans and machines is a better model for companies to explore. Imagine the impact of every worker in your organization being assisted by a team of AIs and bots. Think of it as a cloud- and app-enhanced workforce whose every time-consuming task is partly automated and optimized.

We don't have to look far to find an example of this model at work. During the last few years, McDonald's has experimented with digital ordering kiosks in some of its restaurants. Instead of driving up to a window or walking up to a cashier, patrons place their orders at a friendly touchscreen. No human interaction occurs. There also is, presumably, no line either (or at least less of one). Customers pick their items, confirm their orders, pay, get their receipts, and wait to be called. The orders are sent to the food preparation team, and, moments later, the meals are ready to pick up. Pretty simple, right? And yet, this process makes a lot of people uncomfortable. Why? Because they see a retail function once performed by people being handled by machines. Okay. Fair enough. But is that really what has happened?

As it happens, we've spent some time observing some of the earliest McDonald's locations where kiosks were put into service, most notably in Europe. What we saw wasn't necessarily a reduction in staff, but a reshuffling of staff. Cashiers, who were no longer swamped with customers placing orders, focused on other tasks, like customer service, the expediting of orders, cleaning off tables, and restocking supplies. Their jobs weren't eliminated. Their jobs shifted from taking orders to managing orders and customer experiences outside of the automated ordering process itself. This isn't to say that some McDonald's locations haven't taken advantage of the boost in efficiency to eliminate a few jobs or shortened some staff hours, but that's a management decision. It doesn't have to be that way. The locations we observed were busy, even more so with the introduction of the kiosks, which evidently reduced ordering and wait times by enough of a margin that order volume actually increased. That increase in net revenue and customer visits, even with kiosks, suggests that cashiers-turned-customer service managers were unlikely to be dismissed.

Another example, if you haven't experienced the McDonald's kiosks, is how airlines have introduced touchscreen kiosks in airports. The airline industry adopted the model because it works. Ten years ago, travelers had to get in line, walk up to an airline representative, present their ID and travel information, and be issued a boarding pass. Today most of that process is handled through a kiosk. No human interaction is needed. Has this eliminated jobs? Not necessarily. What it has done is shortened lines and accelerated the check-in process for travelers. Next time you're at an airport, look over your shoulder as your boarding pass is printing and see how many airline representatives are at their ticketing stations. Two? Three? Four? How many used to be there back when we all had to wait in line to be handed a boarding pass by a person? Two? Three? Four?

Automation can replace human jobs, but it doesn't have to. It also can be used to improve customer experiences, enhance productivity, and refocus human workers on more important tasks, from customer service and project management to content creation and team building.

These disruptions, when combined, force organizations to fundamentally rethink their org charts. With contractors and gig workers coming in and out of projects, with mobile workers leveraging collaboration software and new cross-functional methodologies to erode silos, and automation transforming and redefining job functions, the org chart as we once knew it must evolve. This evolution is in part to reflect the reality of the new, more digital, flatter, more agile, and less siloed workplace, but it also reflects non-human participants tasked with performing functions once done by human workers. That's right! Org charts should include bots and AIs, self-service kiosks, and digital assistants. As orgs continue to hybridize this way, and assign tasks and functions to non-human workers, the org chart can't just look "flatter." It also has to start including non-human workers and resources. We realize that this may seem a little strange now, but, five years from now, it won't. This book is about futureproofing your organization. Thinking ahead and skating to where the puck will be rather than where it is now (thanks to hockey legend Wayne Gretzky for the analogy), is the point of this entire exercise. And if you aren't thinking about how different your org chart will look five, 10, or 15 years from now and how smart automation will impact the structure of that org chart, you are missing a big piece of the futureproofing equation.

NEW PARADIGMS OF MOTIVATION, MANAGEMENT AND PERFORMANCE EXPECTATIONS: ADDRESSING THE CURRENT EMPLOYEE ENGAGEMENT CRISIS

Employee productivity, engagement and retention always present challenges for companies of all industries and sizes. These challenges are even greater today when organizations find themselves under more pressure than ever to drive productivity, profitability and growth with fewer resources each year. The global trend toward "doing more with less" has left organizations and their HR departments stretched thin, leaving employees to manage increasingly stressful professional environments that ask more of them than they receive in return. Millennials and digital natives aside, this is not a recipe for success no matter what generation you happen to be dealing with.

Part of the problem is, even with the relief provided by digital productivity tools, the majority of workers across virtually every industry still manage larger workloads than they did just a decade ago. They also are expected to work longer hours and don't think their wages have risen proportionally. Whether we are heading toward a breaking point or an inflection point isn't yet clear, but it is worth noting what kind of impact this combination of high stress and low workplace gratification is having on overall employee engagement.

A 2015 Gallup study [3] revealed the extent to which this has become problematic. Only 31 percent of employees (less than a third) are engaged at work, according to the study. Meanwhile, the other two thirds are either passively disengaged (51 percent) or actively disengaged (17.5 percent).

Here are those numbers side-by-side to convey their severity:

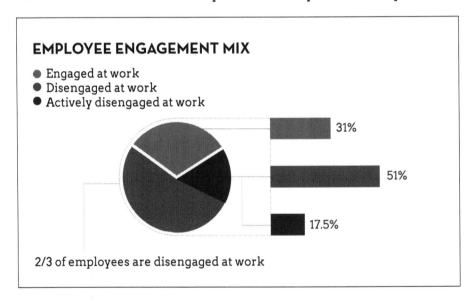

EMPLOYEE ENGAGEMENT MIX

● Engaged at work
● Disengaged at work
● Actively disengaged at work

31%

51%

17.5%

2/3 of employees are disengaged at work

THE MILLENNIAL ENGAGEMENT GAP

Gallup's generational segmentation revealed that, of that 31 percent group of engaged employees, millennials are the least engaged, with 28.9 percent. This compared to Gen X & Boomers, which, combined, balance the equation at 32.9 percent). This insight is important because millennials will account for roughly 75 percent of the global

[3]Adkins, Amy. "Majority of U.S. Employees Not Engaged Despite Gains in 2014." *Gallup*, 28 Jan. 2015.

workforce by 2025. If nothing is done to reverse this trend, it will be excruciatingly difficult for companies whose employees are 71 percent disengaged to be successful in an increasingly competitive global market.

As we have observed in every industry, employee engagement is one of the most critical factors contributing to overall success and to an organization's ability to innovate, adapt to change, identify and pursue emerging market opportunities, and build loyal communities of users and customers. What this means is that low employee engagement doesn't just inflict high turnover rates and productivity losses. Low employee engagement also severely hinders a company's ability to be competitive in a highly dynamic and disruptive economy. If a highly engaged workforce is an asset, and a less-than-engaged workforce is a liability, it stands to reason that finding ways of creating an engaged workforce should be a priority for all companies hoping to compete in the complex and fast-paced 21st century economy.

WHAT IS WORKPLACE GAMIFICATION?

Workplace gamification is a process by which game design and game mechanics are applied to a professional environment and its systems to engage and motivate employees to achieve specific goals.

These goals can be personal goals, company goals or a combination of both. The goals typically rely on common human motivators like competition, collaboration, achievement, status, altruism, and sense of community. Typically, game mechanics rely on challenges, points, levels, badges, and leaderboards to incentivize and reward users. But, when applied to the workplace, other forms of incentives like cash bonuses, advancement opportunities, physical awards, outward recognition, and specialized training are added into the gamification layer.

Workplace gamification is no different from other categories of gamification except it focuses on workplace-related objectives. These objectives can range from helping employees improve job-related skills to boosting their overall productivity. Sales spiffs and contests are common versions of traditional workplace gamification, but digital technologies now provide organizations with a plethora of options to embed gamification as an identifiable and purpose-driven layer into every aspect of their employees' functions. Before devising a plan though, and before technologies and gamification programs can be properly evaluated, the organization must determine specifically what outcomes it wants to drive. The more relevant the outcomes, the more effective and valuable the gamification layer will be. Basically, we are talking about goal setting.

- What are we trying to accomplish?

- What needles are we trying to move?

- What problems are we trying to solve?

- What successes are we trying to scale, build on or improve?

These four questions form the crux of the initial round of discussions that must take place, at the overall company level and at the departmental, line of business (LoB), or team levels. As workplace gamification's purpose is to drive positive behaviors and curb negative ones, it is vital to begin the process by making a list of goals, objectives and even targets that are the focus of the program. The more measurable the goals, the better.

It is important for every silo, group and tribe in the organization to go through this process in addition to the company's overall discussion about goals, objectives and targets. This is because, while some objectives may apply to the organization as a whole, and need to be deployed company-wide, many have to focus on smaller, more localized points. Each department and team has its own set of problems to solve and successes to build on. These also have to be identified to incorporate them into the program.

One way to separate these two categories of goals and objectives is to divide them into Macro Objectives (pertaining to the entire company) and Micro Objectives (pertaining to specific elements of the company).

DEFINING MACRO OBJECTIVES AND MICRO OBJECTIVES

Macro Objectives are objectives that are applicable and relevant to every member of the organization, from the CEO on down to the most junior hire. Another way to look at this category is to think of these objectives as *generalist* objectives, as opposed to objectives relating to specialized skills.

EXAMPLES OF MACRO OBJECTIVES

- **Deep onboarding:** Help employees gain a better understanding of what the company does as a whole and how it does it. Make all the puzzle pieces fit.

- **Resource optimization:** Help employees connect with peers they haven't met yet whose skills and expertise may help them succeed.

- **Career advancement:** Help employees develop leadership skills at their own pace.

- **Improve productivity:** Help employees learn and apply effective time management skills, teach them how to become power users of the company's general purpose technology solutions, and create structure around common activities like project planning, creative ideation, process optimization, and project management.

- **Reduce internal friction:** Help employees learn how to communicate effectively in professional environments.

- **Build a teamwork culture:** Help employees learn how to work better as a team than by themselves.

- **Eliminate toxic behaviors:** Help employees identify harassment and other negative behaviors, then deal with them appropriately.

- **Increase wellness:** Empower employees to improve their diets, activity levels and stress levels.

EXAMPLES OF MICRO OBJECTIVES

Micro Objectives refer to objectives related to specialized functions. Unlike the Macro/generalist objectives, these relate to specific skillsets, departmental needs or role-based activities. Here are a few examples:

- **Improve develop deep skillsets**: Help employees deepen their practical knowledge of key technology solutions unique to their roles and/or function_like CRM, CMS, inventory management systems, data monitoring, billing, etc._by gamifying training.

- **Manufacturing**: Help employees improve safety and reduce the risk of accidents on the production floor.

- **Shipping**: Help employees learn how to minimize damage to products during the shipping process.

- **Digital Marketing**: Help employees post content to digital channels and reply to comments throughout the day to improve breadth and consistency of engagement across digital channels.

- **Sales**: Help employees build stronger relationships with customers, close more deals, and sell more.

- **Customer service and support**: Help employees resolve tickets faster, and improve customer satisfaction.

DEFINING SHORT-TERM AND LONG-TERM OBJECTIVES

Once objectives and goals are identified, the second step in the process is to divide them in terms of short-term and long-term objectives. For the interest of simplicity, it is best to avoid medium-term goals and objectives. Make objectives either short term or long term. As a rule of thumb, any target set along a monthly, quarterly or half year timeline should be considered short term. Anything with a 12 month outlook or longer should be considered long term.

Note that setting short-term milestones and intermediate goals on monthly and quarterly timelines can help drive long-term goals. It makes sense to break down long-term goals into small portions, like steps on a flight of stairs. The long-term goal doesn't stop being a long-term goal. It merely informs the creation of a subset of intermediate goals which fall into the short-term goal category.

BRINGING CLARITY TO A COMPLEX MODEL

Once macro and micro objectives are identified and divided into short- and long-term quadrants, the next step is to map them. Using a simple graph divided between macro, micro, short-term, and long-term quadrants is ideal.

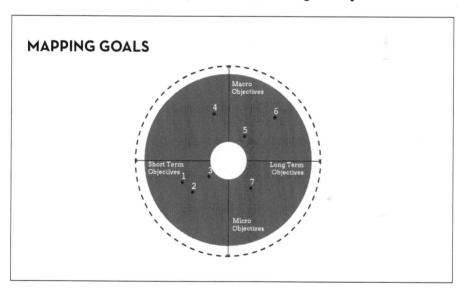

MAPPING GOALS

In the above chart, Objectives 1, 2 and 3 represent short-term micro objectives, Objective 4 represents a short-term macro objective, Objectives 5 and 6 represent long-term macro objectives, and Objective 7 represents a long-term micro objective.

As you begin to graph micro objectives from all of the company's departments, teams and roles, you may want to color-code those objectives. Being able to identify who they relate to will help you effectively incorporate them into the program later.

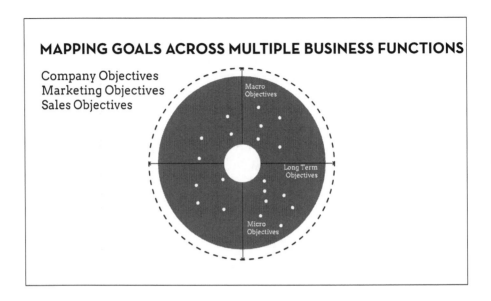

MAPPING GOALS ACROSS MULTIPLE BUSINESS FUNCTIONS

Company Objectives
Marketing Objectives
Sales Objectives

Macro
Objectives

Long Term
Objectives

Micro
Objectives

APPLYING GAMIFICATION TO THE THREE PERIODS OF THE EMPLOYEE LIFECYCLE

An important dimension of workplace gamification relates to the three periods of an employee lifecycle: *employee acquisition, employee development* and *long term employee retention*. Put another way, workplace gamification also should be divided into three general categories, each targeting a particular mission relating to employee lifecycle management:

1. Attracting employees,

2. Developing employees and

3. Retaining employees.

Working with HR professionals, organizations should strive to answer the following questions:

• How can we use gamification to help attract, recruit and onboard new talent?

- How can we use gamification to help develop our existing employees into being happier, more effective, more productive, and more engaged than they already are?

- How can we use gamification to keep our best employees from leaving?

Objectives (both *micro* and *macro*) tend to vary and evolve depending on where an employee happens to be in his or her employee lifecycle. For instance, macro objectives relating to recruiting and onboarding will tend to focus on helping a prospect and/or new hire learn the basics about the company—gain an appreciation for the company's values and policies, understand job expectations, partner with peers who will shadow them during these first few critical weeks, learn how to access resources, and adjust to their new role. Once they reach the development phase of their journey, those macro objectives will transition from introduction to improvement.

Designing workplace gamification without taking into account the need to address all three lifecycle missions—acquisition, development and retention—ultimately is doomed to produce limited results. For maximum effect, workplace gamification has to focus on all three.

INCORPORATING GOALS MAPPING INTO EMPLOYEE ACQUISITION, DEVELOPMENT AND RETENTION

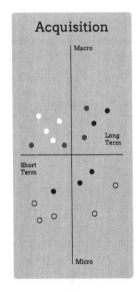

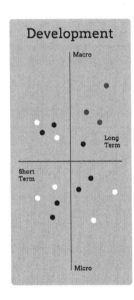

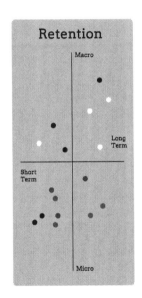

HOW ARE COMPANIES ALREADY USING WORKPLACE GAMIFICATION TO ATTRACT EMPLOYEES?

Several years ago, PricewaterhouseCoopers (PwC) realized that most job candidates in one of its European markets spent less than 15 minutes on its career website before their interviews. As a result, candidates arrived unprepared, resulting in a less-than-ideal experience for them and PwC recruiters. Onboarding for those who were hired was also an area PwC sought to improve, and it turned to gamification to address these two issues.

PwC created a game called "MultiPoly," which made learning about the company and its culture more fun and interactive than viewing a traditional career website. The result was that job applicants spent up to 90 minutes playing MultiPoly (nine time longer than the 10 minutes they previously spent on the website), which gave them a more thorough understanding of the company, its culture, and what to expect from the interview and beyond. As the game helped candidates familiarize themselves with the company, it ultimately improved candidate selection, interview performance and post-hire onboarding process as well. The game ended its run in 2016, but its success endures as a case study in recruitment gamification and adaptable proof of the concept for other companies.

HOW ARE COMPANIES ALREADY USING GAMIFICATION TO DEVELOP EMPLOYEES?

We've already touched on the opportunity to use gamification to help employees develop deep skillsets relating to specific technology solutions. This can be especially important for companies struggling with technology deployments and implementation. For instance, given that half of all CRM deployments ultimately fail, using gamification to help tip the scales of CRM implementation success in a company's favor makes good business sense. Gamification platforms like Badgeville and Bunchball were quick to seize on the opportunity, creating modular gamification layers for some of the world's most popular business platforms. Among them: Salesforce, Jive, SAP Jam and SuccessFactors Learning, NICE Workforce Optimization, BMC's RemedyForce, Yammer, Sharepoint, IBM Connections, Zendesk, Lithium, Workday, Wordpress, and Skillsoft.

Though results vary from one company to the next, adding a gamification layer to these platforms results in across-the-board improvements. Here is a short list of commonly reported categories of improvements curated from Badgeville and Bunchball case studies involving the above platforms:

- Increase in technology adoption,

- Accelerated technology adoption,

- Increase in revenue per user,

- Accelerated learning,

- Increase in user engagement,

- Improved compliance,

- Improved data accuracy,

- Increase in new deals/sales,

- Accelerated sales cycles,

- Increase in forecast accuracy,

- Increase in collaboration,

- Increase in user productivity,

- Improved partner management (channel),

- Improvements in customer service and support, and

- Increase in user/employee motivation.

HOW CAN COMPANIES USE GAMIFICATION TO RETAIN EMPLOYEES?

It would be dishonest to claim that technology alone will help most companies reduce their employee turnover rate and retain their best people. Gamification alone won't do it, just like hefty bonuses and company perks won't necessarily achieve that outcome either. The truth is that employee retention, especially in the long term, poses a major challenge for almost all businesses.

Reasons that motivate employees to stay tend to exist on a spectrum. Each reason has a different position along that spectrum for each individual employee. For some, high pay will be at the top of the list. For others, status and recognition are more important than money. Also on the list of reasons people stay with a company are pride in the company or one's job title, a sense of purpose, having a positive impact on the world, great health benefits, location, flexible hours, pet-friendly offices, easy access to a gym, and free products. A great boss and team, a fun environment, challenging problems to solve, amazing clients, and a culture of innovation and ideas come together to create cultures that make employees love what they do, love who they do it with and for, and love where they get to do it every day. The more of these motivators a company can string together, the more likely that company will be to retain its employees.

What we are talking about is culture, and, specifically, a culture focused on retention. Companies that understand the building blocks of a culture of retention and take time to implement them typically enjoy high retention rates. Culture comes first and gamification second. In other words, gamification cannot be treated as a shortcut when it comes to helping companies improve employee retention. It has to be used as an internal amplification tool for *existing* cultures of retention. Cart before horse.

How does a company know if they have a culture focused on retention? Here are a few strong indicators:

- Companies that look for ways to reward employees for the right behaviors and outcomes.

- Companies that offer employees opportunities for growth, training and advancement.

- Companies that do everything they can to empower their employees to be active participants in the company's growth and success.

Companies that reflect any or all of these traits will have a much easier time integrating a gamification layer into their existing cultures of retention, especially in comparison to companies that haven't taken the time to build these foundations.

Once a company understands the full range of motivators that drive long-term employee retention, the next step is to incorporate those motivators into their gamification program. What would that list look like?

Here is an example:

- **Financial:** Create contests with financial rewards.

- **Fun environment:** Inject short (three minute) games into an employee's day to help them de-stress.

- **Sense of purpose:** Create daily quizzes that emphasize the company's impact on the world or an industry. Include charitable giving and philanthropic causes the company is involved with.

- **Great coworkers:** Inject a team/collaborative dimension into the gamification layer to promote teamwork, collaboration and esprit de corps. (Think of Pokémon Go's red, blue and yellow teams, for instance, or Hogwarts' houses in the Harry Potter series.)

- **Innovation and ideas:** Incorporate problem solving and puzzles into the gamification layer.

- **Competition:** Test employees on their knowledge of the company and its industry.

- **Advancement and opportunities:** Use gamification to help employees accelerate their corporate learning, sharpen their skills, and create paths to certification and advancement.

- **Great boss:** Create bonus rounds in which an employee can virtually partner with their boss or another executive to score additional points and/or unlock special rewards.

- **Loyalty:** Reward employees with streak, longevity, and comeback rewards and bonuses. Create bonus games, levels and rewards (digital and real-world) that can be unlocked only after they have been with the company for a certain amount of time.

By creating a range of games and activities that touch on as many retention motivators as possible, a company's gamification layer can make gamification relevant and engaging for a large percentage of a company's workforce and reinforce the factors that ultimately help drive employee retention.

In addition, gamification, when designed and executed properly, can help employees feel more empowered and in charge of their own careers and success by facilitating goal setting, providing performance feedback and accelerating e-learning. For employees, especially those who may feel the itch to move on, having tools in place that give them unique reasons to stay can be the difference between losing or retaining a valuable asset.

THE IMPORTANCE OF REWARDS AND INCENTIVES

For the sake of simplicity, incentives can be divided into four distinct categories:

1. Compensation incentives, like bonuses, raises and permanent employee perks.

2. Reward incentives, like cash prizes, non-cash prizes and awards.

3. Appreciation incentives, like company parties and special events.

4. Recognition incentives, which focus on establishing status and social standing within the company.

To illustrate the range of the *reward incentives* categories, which usually represent the lion's share of gamification incentives, note that digital achievement badges *and* real-world sales spiffs fall into this category.

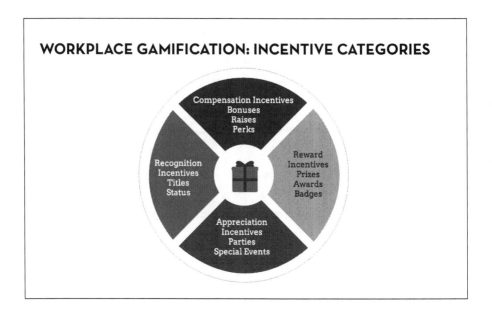

WORKPLACE GAMIFICATION: INCENTIVE CATEGORIES

It is also important to remember that. in organizations where improving collaboration, teamwork, and group cohesion are stated objectives, incentives *also* should reward team and group performance, not only individual performance. We already mentioned *Pokémon Go*'s red, blue and yellow teams, as well as the Hogwarts' houses (from the *Harry Potter* books) as examples of how to create a team ecosystem within the gamification layer.

We recommend that you sit down with developers and gamification solutions providers to discuss how to allow employees to join groups and teams within the gamification layer, both symmetrically and asymmetrically.

Symmetric teams are based on the company's org chart. If Bob works as a digital business development rep on Jane's sales team, and that team belongs to the software sales group, then Bob's profile in the gamification layer should be attached to Jane's digital business development team *and* the software sales group. This will make it easier to batch gamification achievements together by team and group, allowing leaders to calculate group contest winners and analyze performance at the team and group levels (which we will talk a little more about in a few moments). Asymmetric teams are not based on the company's org chart.

They are random. Their purpose is to create *esprit de corps* and collaboration across silos, which is an important component of workplace gamification. As important as it is to use gamification to drive cohesion and common purpose within working teams and departments, it is equally important to ensure that, in doing so, the company doesn't reinforce a silo-based entrenchment mentality. Bringing asymmetric teams into the gamification mix creates a vehicle by which employee collaboration and cohesion are expanded beyond silos, rewarded and encouraged. On the company wide level (a macro-objective), leveraging workplace gamification to create connective tissue and a broader, silo-agnostic team mentality across the company is vital to the growth and health of a company culture. A good example of where team asymmetry can work well is a health and wellness program where common goals aren't necessarily tied to departmental objectives. Team symmetry, on the other hand, works better for programs that aim to drive department-centric goals, like unit sales or revenue targets. Unfortunately, principles of team asymmetry often are glossed over to the detriment of company-wide gamification programs.

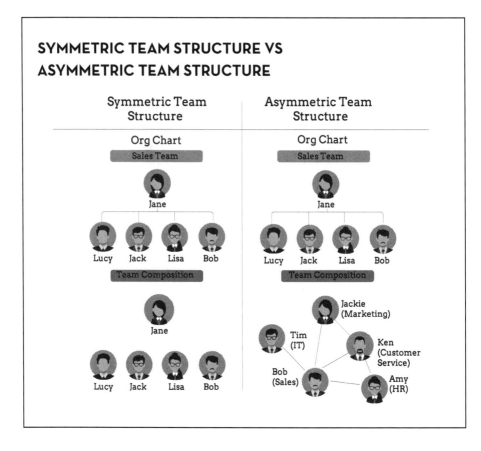

Driving *compensation incentives* is a little more complex than driving *reward incentives* like badges and prizes. Companies should use the gamification layer to create challenges that double as clear paths to advancement. Our quadrant for employee development includes four dimensions:

1. Experience

2. Skills and training

3. Leadership, management and responsibility, and

4. Collaborators, peers and mentors.

THE EMPLOYEE DEVELOPMENT QUADRANT

Challenges built into the gamification layer should target the following four dimensions:

1. Build additional depth and breadth of experience,

2. Reward the acquisition of new skills and the completion of additional training,

3. Create opportunities for leadership, management and responsibility, then tie them to challenges and accomplishment milestones, and

4. Help employees create a network of collaborators, peers and mentors that help propel them forward

However, don't stop there. Workplace gamification is also a social, community-driven ecosystem, and competition drives success. Make paths to success and high achievement visible to all. By making high achievers' milestone achievements and digital badges visible to all, they become flagstones along the path that high achievers tend to follow. Having visibility to this will help other employees looking to follow in their footsteps understand what they have to do in order to move up as well. A final note on incentives, it also is important to layer incentives along short-term and long-term timelines. The employee engagement spectrum, along with employee motivation, requires a mix of short-term and long-term goal setting and achievement. Too much emphasis on short-term challenges will keep employees from setting long-term paths to success, which can work against employee development and retention objectives. Too much emphasis on long-term challenges can have the opposite effect, making achievements and incentives seem too difficult. Combining short-term and long-term incentives will keep employees engaged and motivated on a daily basis, and their short-term success will help bridge the gap between where they are today and where they may wish to be a year from now. Remember, feedback is important. Integrating ongoing collaboration and communication into a gamification strategy can help strike the right balance between short- and long-term incentive values.

MAPPING COMPANYWIDE GAMIFICATION

Now that we have covered the fundamental elements of workplace gamification planning, it is time to put all of the pieces together. The diagram below *(fig. 8)* is an example of how a fully developed workplace gamification plan should look. It incorporates all of the principles we covered, and organizes the gamification ecosystem into three layers: 1) the POV (point of view) layer at the center, 2) the OD (objective dimension) layer around it and 3) a technology layer that outlines what combination of solutions enable the program function.

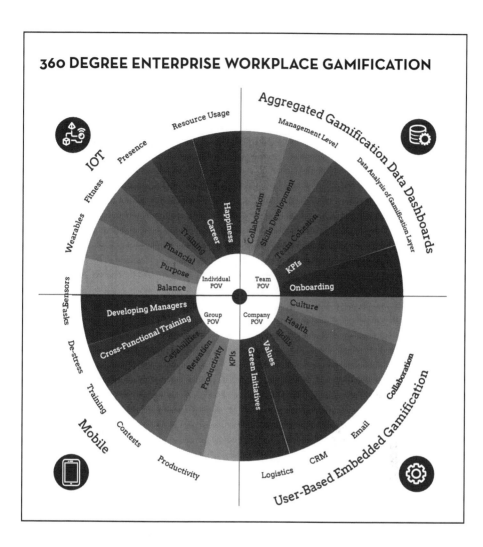

In this example, the company's workplace gamification planning has evolved from the basic dual *macro* and *micro* objective model we introduced earlier to a more enterprise-focused model, adapted to the complexity of a large corporate ecosystem.

Instead of macro and micro objectives, we find a POV layer composed of four levels of focus:

1. Individual,

2. Team,

3. Group, and

4. Company focus.

Note the progression from individual to team, then from team to group, then from group to company. In this context, micro and macro are not absolute categories of objectives, but instead exist on a spectrum. Dividing this core layer into four levels allows the organization to simultaneously address the needs of their individual employees, the teams they work in, the groups that manage the teams, and the company's overall needs without creating interference or confusion in the gamification planning, process and management. Under this model, each key building block of the organization helps develop its own layer of objectives, motivators and games.

THE INDIVIDUAL POV QUADRANT

The OD layer outlines the specific objectives and motivators pursued by each segment of the POV layer. In *Figure 8*, we see that the section of the OD layer that serves the *Individual POV* quadrant focuses on:

- Happiness,

- Career advancement,

- Advanced training,

- Financial rewards,

- Sense of purpose, and

- Work-life balance.

Note that this is only an example, not a definitive list. Companies and their employees should explore what other objectives and motivators apply to them. Each company is unique and should treat this process accordingly.

THE TEAM POV QUADRANT

In our example, we see that the section of the OD layer that serves the *Team POV* quadrant focuses on:

- Boosting collaboration,

- Developing deep/specialized skills,

- Fostering team cohesion,

- Helping the team deliver key KPIs, and

- Improving the onboarding of new teammates.

These team-specific objectives and points of focus may not be immediately clear to a group or departmental manager, which is why our hypothetical company elected to create a team-level POV quadrant. Segmenting gamification to both match *and* address the needs of specific organizational layers is the kind of thinking that will help you properly integrate gamification across your entire company.

THE GROUP POV QUADRANT

Next in our example is the OD layer that serves the *Group POV* quadrant. Again, the objectives listed here are different from those found at the team level. They are:

- Developing competent managers,

- Rewarding cross-functional training,

- Expanding group capabilities,

- Improving retention,

- Increasing productivity, and

- Driving key group KPIs.

Group and departmental objectives, while not divorced from team-level objectives, tend to be slightly more strategic in nature. Whereas team-level objectives may focus more on teamwork and tactical efficiency, group and departmental objectives tend to focus more on big picture organizational improvements, logistic considerations and scalable efficiency.

THE COMPANY POV QUADRANT

Lastly, we come to the OD layer that serves the company as a whole, the *Company POV* quadrant. In our example, its focus is:

- Helping nurture the company's culture across the entire organization,

- Promoting fitness-related activities and healthy lifestyles,

- Building a skilled, entrepreneurial and competent workforce,

- Helping ensure that every new hire finds the right fit in the organization,

- Injecting the company's core values (i.e., ethics, innovation, fearlessness, mutual respect) into employees' everyday lives, and

- Recruiting employees into the company's carbon footprint reduction program.

These objectives are as macro as they get: The focus here is on the relationship between every employee and the company as a whole. Group- and team-level objectives are left to the team layer and the group layer, allowing the company to focus on creating an environment in which groups, teams and individuals can work to the best of their abilities.

The third and final layer is the technology layer, and it deserves its own section.

TECHNOLOGY'S ROLE IN WORKPLACE GAMIFICATION

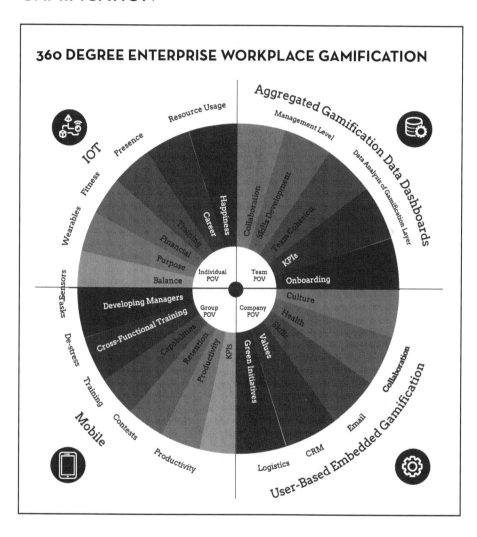

360 DEGREE ENTERPRISE WORKPLACE GAMIFICATION

Let's break the technology layer into four categories:

1. Mobile-enabled gamification,

2. IoT-enabled gamification,

3. User based embedded gamification, and

4. Aggregate gamification data dashboards.

Mobile-enabled gamification simply refers to mobile-compatible and mobile-specific gamification apps. These either live in a mobile app or can be accessed through it. If you are familiar with *Foursquare*, *Pokémon Go* or fitness app *Strava*, you already understand the relationship between gamification and mobility. As mobile devices increasingly become employees' primary professional tools and technology vendors continue shifting to *mobile first* strategies, productivity, collaboration, e-learning, product management, and task management tools will continue migrating from the desktop to mobile devices. The gamification layer is, therefore, increasingly finding its way back into the world of mobility that helped shape it in the first place. This shift creates a natural synergy between mobile-friendly gamification and enterprise software vendors building their interfaces for mobile devices. We are confident that by 2020, gamification relating to job training, internal contests, productivity, task management, e-learning, resource management, and collaboration will be designed for mobile devices.

If you are familiar with *FitBit* and *Garmin* fitness wearables, you already understand the basics of *IoT-enabled gamification*. Wearable sensors collect data about your activity levels and athletic performance (like how many steps you've taken today, or how many miles you ran and how fast) and give you the option to use that data in a gamified setting where you can set goals, collect points toward rewards, or challenge yourself and friends to friendly competitions. Fitness app *Strava*, which we mentioned above, creates a gamification layer for Garmin users with which they earn achievement badges. The badges are based on the number of miles they swam, biked or ran that month, how fast they completed a particular segment, or how well they finished a workout against the group they were training with. While many companies are subsidizing the purchase of fitness trackers and wearables for their employees, incorporating IoT-driven fitness gamification into their corporate wellness programs, the same principles guiding the individual and social gamification of fitness can be applied to other types of performances and KPIs outside of sports.

By combining wearables, mobile devices and sensors, workplace gamification also can be applied to the improvement of manufacturing and production efficiency, warehouse management, shipping and deliveries, facility resource management, power usage, collaboration, fleet management, and employee engagement. IoT-driven gamification can, for instance, be used to help employees save energy throughout the day. Then programs can be developed to reward individuals and teams for helping the company reduce its carbon footprint. Sensors detecting that a conference room or shared space is unoccupied and isn't booked for another hour can prompt a nearby manager to organize an impromptu 10- to 15 minute team meeting to brainstorm about something or give her feedback on an idea. By rewarding managers for organizing these types of team-building exercises, IoT-enabled gamification can help address team-level objectives like the ones we outlined in our earlier example:

• Boosting collaboration,

• Fostering team cohesion and

• Helping deliver key team KPIs.

Purpose drives all good design, and workplace gamification is no different in that regard. IoT-enabled gamification has the potential to add spontaneity to the gamification layer, which is a positive attribute to game dynamics and a physical dimension to workplace gamification that screen-based gamification (PC and mobile) sometimes fail to deliver. Being able to have objects, rooms and even entire buildings interact with employees and play a role in workplace gamification opens up a world of employee engagement and workplace efficiency possibilities for game designers, managers and business planners.

User-based embedded gamification refers to the workplace gamification layer that each individual user sees. "User-based" refers to user-level screens showing things like task and challenge completions, achievements and awards, levels and scores, digital badges, and team, group and company rankings. "Embedded" refers to the extent to which software vendors like Badgeville and Bunchball can embed their gamification layer into popular enterprise software from companies like Salesforce, Jive, SAP, Lithium, IBM, and Microsoft. Why do we mention it? Because it is only half of the story. There is also a top-down *aggregate* view of a company's workplace gamification ecosystem, and we are going to talk about that next.

Aggregate gamification data dashboards refer to the executive's view of a company's entire gamification ecosystem. Think of them as management dashboards that combine all of the organization's gamification data and analyze it in real time to do things like graph trends, identify outliers and opportunities, and rate winners and losers. Here are some of the things this kind of top-down aggregate view allows decision makers to see:

- Which groups contribute the most to the company's carbon footprint reduction initiative.

- Which teams systematically show the greatest amount of dedication to team cohesion and collaboration.

- Which individuals show the most interest in e-learning and skills development.

- Which sales teams have the most competitive spirit.

- Which facilities have managed to systematically reduce workplace accidents by more than 50 percent YoY.

- Which group managers and team leads appear to be more effective and motivated leaders.

- Which groups respond better to recognition incentives than financial rewards.

- Which groups enjoy the company's highest employee retention rates.

- Which teams systematically demonstrate the highest onboarding success rates.

- Which group appears to produce the greatest amount of motivated leaders in the company.

On the one hand, giving leadership teams an opportunity to monitor the success of their gamification ecosystem at a general *and* a granular level is a good way of illustrating and quantifying its value. Like any investment, it pays to measure its ROI based on the aggregate value of its impact on overall productivity gains, lower employee turnover, uplifts in employee engagement, and other specific objectives identified within the organization.

On the other hand, being able to identify what internal strategies and tactics work and don't work, allows decision makers to quickly shift from low-performing to high-performing models, and scale them across the rest of the organization. It also gives decision makers the ability to identify outstanding individuals, high-performing teams and gifted leaders that might have otherwise gotten lost in the day-to-day shuffle or passed over by inattentive management layers between annual performance reviews.

Data is power. One of the natural byproducts of workplace gamification is data—loads of data on everything from employee morale and group performance to hidden innovation clusters and internal program ROI. Access to this kind of data has the potential to drive internal opportunity discovery *and* better decision making. It also is important to mention that a successful UX for gamification makes use of data visualization to make it easier for managers to spot the performers, whereas raw data, like simple numbers or scores, often fail to do so.

For these reasons, it is vital for senior executives and program managers to ensure that the gamification technology they invest in provides them with a top-down view, layered parsing and actionable analysis of the data it collects. The same focus applied to market and customer data should be applied to organizational and employee data. They are two sides of the same coin.

HOW DOES WORKPLACE GAMIFICATION FIT IN OUR FUTUREPROOFING EQUATION?

Although the value of workplace gamification as a technology investment may still seem murky for a lot of traditionally-minded decision makers, it is key to understanding how to recruit, develop and retain engaged, skilled and talented employees. It is also at the core of ensuring that a company's workforce remains aligned with the organization's goals and focused on delivering on its objectives.

Work is work, but work can be fun. Challenges sometimes mean more when they are clearly defined as achievements to pursue rather than obstacles to overcome. By creating a game-like structure around the workplace that includes fair and simple rules, clearly-marked milestones, shared accountability, achievement rewards, healthy competition, and social cohesion, this methodology can be used to correct negative behaviors and drive positive behaviors.

Organizations can use gamification to build stronger, more positive and enduring corporate cultures, which tend to become more efficient, adaptable, open to new challenges, and, therefore, far more likely to handle change and disruption with the right mindset.

Organizations can organize, analyze and give shape to their internal ecosystems somewhat organically by focusing on individual employee acquisition, development and retention; team development and cohesion; group optimization and efficiency, and the reinforcement of companywide values. Gamification helps with self-management. It creates well-defined lanes, conspicuous paths to advancement, access to resources and solutions to problems, and paths over or around career obstacles. Instead of pursuing athletic goals, like they might if they were using Garmin Connect or Strava, employees pursue professional ones. They can be task, project- or skill-building based, or pretty much anything the organization needs them to be.

Gamification also can help build bridges between silos. It can help connect employees to each other on a more social and natural level. It can focus on work-related goals, but it also can form and reinforce social bonds, and promote collaboration and the exchange of ideas. In many ways, workplace gamification, if used correctly, can become a structural and technology cornerstone in the humanization of business.

The humanization business, which was an important topic of discussion at the height of social media's transformation into what eventually became "social business," is still a competitive goal worth pursuing, and one that fits well in the futureproofing equation. The humanization of business, which ultimately drives loyalty and trust in customers and employees alike, is one of the more subtle but potentially rewarding opportunities that digital transformation can deliver to customer-centric companies. The humanization of business also sets winners apart from also-in companies in most industries. Nobody likes to be a number. Anything a company can do to create a culture of humanization is a net positive.

Workplace gamification also fits into the world of digital transformation at the IT level as it requires a combination of Big Data, cloud computing, mobility, IoT, and cognitive computing to deliver its full potential. Workplace gamification cannot be achieved effectively and at scale outside of a proactive and somewhat mature digital transformation program. Workplace gamification should be approached much in the same way that Ally approached its own digital transformation, with real focus and under the supervision of at least one C-level leader.

It seems obvious that human resources should take the lead on this and partner with IT to create this new internal model, but this requires that HR's leadership be elevated to C-level status. Chief employee officer, chief human resources officer, chief culture officer... the title doesn't matter as long as HR is tasked and empowered to drive this change, and to actively take charge of nurturing, developing and preparing the workforce for what comes next. By creating an ecosystem of internal opportunities driven by clear incentives and rewards, then injecting it with a sense of community that drives to the heart of an organization's shared journey and common sense of purpose, companies can transform their human resources program into an engine of opportunity.

From what we have seen, the successful deployment of this kind of change depends on the extent to which an organization with a clear vision for what it wants its employees to be able to accomplish can communicate that vision to its HR department, IT department and gamification technology providers. The organizational vision must drive the technology discussion, not the other way around. Objectives and goals always come before the technology and tools. Technology and tools are the means to an end, not the end unto themselves. Organizations also should strive to strike the right balance between value to the employee and what is essentially a form of automated micromanagement. None of this should feel like micromanagement.

It should feel to employees like empowerment. The goal is to Provide each employee a personal dashboard that helps them be more productive, engaged, plugged in, aware of opportunities, empowered to make their own course corrections, and serves as a gateway to e-learning and continuous improvement training.

One caveat to note is that as this sort of system collects data through apps, mobile devices, wearables and sensors, companies should be sensitive to their employees' privacy concerns. Companies need to be careful not to transform what should feel like an employee-empowering workplace into an intrusive corporate culture whose employees are under constant electronic surveillance. Clarity of purpose, the development of a culture of trust and setting the right mood are vital to the success of this kind of program. It has to be explained honestly and be transparent. Without trust, this kind of model cannot take root.

It also is important to ensure that employees see the value of the gamification layer so they opt into it. Before digital technologies came along, companies used to try and force team-building exercises on their employees. The effort came from a good place, and it was, to some extent, the right idea, but the mandatory nature of these exercises made them unpopular. *Opt-in* models are preferable to mandatory participation models. No one wants to be forced to play a game. It defeats the purpose. Properly designed workplace gamification should create an atmosphere of fun and rewarding competition. The results of gamification programs should be obvious that employees who participate in the program achieve better outcomes than employees who don't. As much as possible, employees should be encouraged to manage their own level of involvement with the gaming aspects of their careers, even while encouraging them to get more involved as they become more comfort with the program.

Programs like this should be built on a foundation of *common mission* and *shared experience*. As much as traditional CEOs may cringe at this insight, it needs to be shared. It's easier to build a community around something fun than around "a job." Real communities are tribes. They form around a central point of passion. It could be a soccer team, road cycling, beautiful industrial design, or the pursuit of monthly bonuses. It doesn't matter what the passion point is as long as at the center of it all you have something people are jointly passionate about. Companies that turn their internal cultures into tribes tend to enjoy much higher levels of employee engagement, productivity, retention, and adaptability. When disruption comes, these are the kinds of employees that will stick around and fight for the company's survival. If you aren't building tribes, you aren't running your company the way it should be.

Engaged employees also create engaged customers. Tribes spread from within your walls to outside your walls. Most futureproof company's' customer behaviors are a direct reflection of their employee behaviors. From IBM, Starbucks and Apple to Ford, Harley Davidson and Ubisoft, tribes are tribes. Happy employees create happy customers. Loyal employees create loyal customers. Smiles are contagious. Confidence in a brand or product is contagious. What you build inside your walls will spread to your market a hundredfold.

For companies struggling to build a sense of community across their organization, companies that have found it difficult to build a internal tribe for their brand, workplace gamification might be the vehicle through which this transformation is achieved.

MOBILITY, FLEXIBILITY AND JOB CUSTOMIZATION

We wrote earlier in this chapter about adjusting to millennial and post-millennial expectations. This may be a good place to reemphasize that futureproofing isn't about millennials or accommodating them. It is about *evolving* into the kind of company that can change and adapt quickly and often. This evolution means getting rid of things that get in the way of what's next.

For IT, it means getting rid of outdated technologies to make room for newer, better ones. For marketing, it means getting rid of outdated models and channels to make room for more effective ones. For customer service, it means... well, it means a lot of work, because the whole model needs to be overhauled. And we just spent a good deal of time outlining how, for HR, it doesn't mean getting rid of aging workers, so don't think that's where we are going with this section. Age doesn't make people obsolete. No company stands to gain the slightest advantage by arbitrarily replacing X'ers and Boomers with millennials. Experience is never a cheap commodity, and companies that treat is as if it were are making a mistake. But HR can help companies get rid of outdated work environments.

No company can futureproof itself if it can't let go of old equipment. Any company that can't let go of old fax machines, 20th century cubicles, boxy old desktop computers, and whatever else already wasn't cutting edge in 1995 is off to a bad start. The old stuff has to go. The old workplace paradigms have to go. Companies have to make room for what's next, and the only way to do that is to let go of everything that doesn't play a part in that transformation. It doesn't matter if you rationalize that replacing old desks and tearing out 20-year-old video conferencing equipment is psychological. Maybe it is. Maybe it isn't. Even if it is, it matters. No millennial will be happy and engaged working in a cluttered, uninspired office that feels stuck in the past. It just isn't going to happen.

There's a place for nostalgia in business. It ties you to a company's roots and history, and there's value in that. It matters that the $20 billion company you work for started out in a garage. It matters that one of your business heroes used to work in the corner office that's now become the main conference room. No one is saying you should erase the past or that it isn't valuable. But clutter isn't valuable. Holding on to the wrong things for the wrong reasons isn't valuable. You want to impress millennials with the company's history? Hang some old photos on the walls. Inject the office decor with some authentic artifacts from back in the day, things everyone can walk by and look at. But forcing people to work in a museum? That doesn't work. It's the wrong environment for progress and futureproofing. You can't effectively futureproof an organization if you can't let go of the past.

So what's the new model? Less clutter. Fewer desk ornaments. More power outlets. Better Wi-Fi. Cooler furniture. More sunlight. Technology hanging from the walls that matches the technology your employees carry in their pockets. Areas where teams can meet informally, with couches and surfaces to rest their drinks and laptops on. Fewer conference rooms and more collaboration hubs. It's a more mobile-friendly workplace. A friendlier feeling workplace, where collaboration can feel like "hanging out," even though it isn't that at all. There's a reason some of the world's most innovative companies have pleasant, friendly, deliberately informal campuses and headquarters. We hate to use the term "cool" in a business book, but creating cool workplaces does tend to drive coolness. A cool office means a cool place to work, and a cool place to work attracts and retains talent. Cool companies create cool products and experiences. Cool breeds cool. We're talking about people in this chapter, not experiences, but if you can't create outstanding work experiences at your company, it's going to be difficult to attract and retain smart, cool, innovative talent.

With this workplace transformation comes a slew of other potential changes. How much of an employee's time can be spent off site, for instance? Millennials like to work from home if they feel like it. They might need to clear their heads and go work at a coffee shop to get away for a few hours. They're still being productive, they just aren't necessarily chained to their desk from nine to five. That's the sort of change that organizations also have to contemplate. How do you manage a workforce that doesn't treat "the office" the same way that X'ers and Boomers do? How do you set rules for this? How do you create mechanisms and infrastructure that give younger employees that kind of flexibility and freedom without losing productivity. How do you keep a handle on data security when half of your employees routinely use public Wi-Fi when they're away from the office and most also use their personal devices for work?

New questions will pop up during the next few years. With silos disappearing and technology seeping into every facet of work, will traditional job titles still apply? Will 20th century vacation and time-off models still make sense? How will employment even be defined if the trend toward hiring independent contractors and gig workers instead of full-time employees continues to disrupt traditional models of employment?

A certain amount of flexibility will be required. Organizations will have to actively consider how innovation and futureproofing also fits in their everyday HR decisions, and the way that work environments will have to adapt to new paradigms of employment and workforce expectations.

STEM, GRAY-COLLAR JOBS AND THE FUTURE OF EMPLOYMENT.

A lot of what we talk about here touches on *the future of work*—how technology disruption shapes how companies will operate as our world transitions from yesterday's old operational models to new ones, run partly on ubiquitous, ambient, intelligent technologies. Understand the future of work isa pretty fundamental piece of mapping out where digital transformation will take us in the next 20 to 30 years.

Instead of *the future of work*, though, which is broad and too far-reaching to adequately lay out in this book, we want to draw your attention to *the future of employment*. Specifically, what type of impact will *advanced industries* and STEM jobs ultimately have on the job market.

STEM stands for Science, Technology, Engineering and Maths. In other words, STEM jobs are "tech" jobs: Material sciences, healthcare research, software development, robotics, high tech maintenance, and so on. We predict that demand for STEM jobs is about to start growing quickly.

This growth results in some questions. Will STEM jobs help drive more economic value than other industries and job categories? Will they force a reboot of how we approach education, including K-12? Will K-12 education and job training merge or will they remain mostly separate? What will be the impact of these changes on the business world? How will companies, large and small, leverage STEM professions to gain a strategic advantage in their respective markets in times of technological disruption? How much of my company's workforce should have a STEM background by 2025, 2030 and 2035? How should my organization integrate STEM jobs into its ecosystem? How many of our executives realistically should have STEM-related competencies as our business becomes increasingly reliant on technology?

These are the types of questions everyone reading this book also should ask. They're hard questions. They force most executives to push past their comfort zones, which is always a good sign. We don't expect anyone to find easy answers to any of them. If you can start thinking about this though, that's a good next step.

To better frame this topic, let's quickly talk about a business sector generally known as *advanced industries*. The term refers to roughly 50 industries heavily centered around STEM and R&D. Among them are wireless telecommunications, computer systems design, automotive, healthcare, aerospace, biotech, and household appliances. Here are a few points about advanced industries:

- Thirty-five of these industries fall into the *manufacturing* sector. (This is important, so make a mental note of it.)

- Twelve qualify as *service* industries (like software publishers, wireless carriers, medical and diagnostic labs, etc.).

- Only three fall into the energy sector. They are: electric power generation, mining, and oil and gas extraction.

First things first, 35 of the 50 advanced industries are in the manufacturing sector. That's more than two thirds. As we note, the impact that the erosion of manufacturing jobs has had on the American middle class and the economic stress it has wreaked on blue collar workers is an insight that always catches our attention. Given how much surplus manufacturing labor the U.S. has, the intersection of U.S. manufacturing and STEM careers is opportunity rich for companies that can figure out how to transition blue collar communities to STEM careers.

Next let's look at some labor statistics for our three advanced industry categories. According to the Brookings Institution, in 2013, those numbers were (rounded up or down for simplicity) [4]:

- Advanced industries – Services (12/50): 6.2 million jobs.

- Advanced industries – Manufacturing (35/50): 5.5 million jobs.

- Advanced industries – Energy (3/50): 700,000 jobs.

---

4 Muro, Mark, et al. *America's Advanced Industries: What They Are, Where They Are, and Why They Matter*. Brookings, February 2015,

That's right! Twelve industries (services) produce more than 35 (manufacturing). It wasn't always so. But consider what's happened to manufacturing in the last 35 to 40 years. We aren't just talking about cheap overseas labor and the commoditization of international shipping. We are talking about manufacturing efficiency. For instance, in 1980, it took 25 jobs to generate $1 million in manufacturing output. Today it only takes maybe five jobs to do that.

Take a moment to absorb that point. Five people can now produce the same output as 25 people just a generation ago. What does that mean? We aren't economists or labor productivity specialists, but it doesn't take a lot of computing power to realize that the next milestone in that evolution of human productivity in manufacturing will be one person generating the manufacturing output of five people. How? Automation, mostly. Smart manufacturing and the industrial IoT (IIoT) will eventually replace most manufacturing jobs. Why robots, you ask? Robots are cheaper to operate and their work is more consistent. For every factory worker whose cost to an employer is $25 per hour, a robot can do the same job for $8 an hour. Five years from now, that $8 might drop even lower.

This doesn't necessarily spell doom for employment in the manufacturing sector, by the way, but it suggests that more displacement of blue collar workers is inevitable. The question then becomes, where do manufacturing workers go next?

Follow one possible logical progression. If you currently work in manufacturing that isn't in an advanced industry, you may want to transition to advanced industry manufacturing sooner rather than later and acquire advanced technology skills while you're there. If you already know that a robot can do your job at least as well as you can (if not better or faster), you may ant to consider transitioning to a role in a related advanced industry *services* field.

This book is not about future-proofing careers. It's about future-proofing businesses, so we are going to flip that script in a minute. Let's look at how fast advanced industry jobs are growing. Again, according to Brookings:

- Advanced industry jobs (U.S.) in 1980: 11.3 million

- Advanced industry jobs (U.S.) in 2000: 11.3 million

- Advanced industry jobs (U.S.) in 2013: 12.3 million

- Advanced industry jobs (U.S.) in 2015: 12.9 million

Compared to U.S. job growth on the whole, that growth curve is fairly anemic:

- Total employment (U.S.) in 1980: 97.5 million

- Total employment (U.S.) in 2000: 135.6 million

- Total employment (U.S.) in 2013: 141.8 million

- Total employment (U.S.) in 2015: 143.1 million

This means advanced industries' share of U.S. jobs has shrunk, not grown, since 1980:

- Advanced industries' share of employment (U.S.) in 1980: 11.6%

- Advanced industries' share of employment (U.S.) in 2000: 8.3%

- Advanced industries' share of employment (U.S.) in 2013: 8.7%

- Advanced industries' share of employment (U.S.) in 2015: 9.0%

This looks like bad news, right? Not so fast. For the same time period, advanced industries' share of *output* has grown, not shrunk. Advanced industries increased their productivity by roughly 2.7 percent a year since 1980, while the rest of the economy increased its average productivity by about 1.4 percent per year for the same timeframe.

Following a similar trend line, advanced industries jobs now average $214,000 per worker worth of output compared with $108,000 for the average worker outside of advanced industries. In addition, while advanced industries only account for less than 10 percent of U.S. jobs, they are responsible for generating a whopping 60 percent of U.S. exports, and their combined output accounted for a massive 17.2 percent of U.S. GDP in 2015. If you're an investor, that's an interesting insight.

Also, earnings for an advanced industries worker averaged $95 thousand in 2015, while workers in other sectors only averaged $53 thousand a year. If you're a job seeker, that is also an interesting bit of insight.

WHY DOES ANY OF THIS MATTER?

For starters, it tells us that advanced industries are likely more attractive to investors and labor, and, by virtue of being STEM-driven, also better equipped to adapt to change than non-advanced industries. Secondly, as we mentioned at the start of this section, advanced industries are made up of 50 industry subsets, 12 of which are advanced service industries. Nearly 80 percent of the advanced industry jobs created between 2013 and 2015 were concentrated in the services subset. Nearly two thirds of that growth was further concentrated in four specific industry categories:

1. Computer systems design,

2. Web search and internet publishing,

3. Software products, and

4. Data processing and hosting.

Do those four industry categories look familiar? They should. They are the sectors driving digital transformation.

WHAT DOES THIS ALL MEAN AND WHAT ARE WE GETTING AT?

There is a shift coming, and it will move most job functions toward technology management skillsets. Regardless of the role—marketing, sales, project management, auto repair, warehouse management, stocking, senior executives, educators, police officers, HR, and so on—everyone will be a technologist. Everyone will be managing bots, AIs, digital assistants, and a layered ecosystem of interconnected technology solutions by 2030. White collar jobs won't just be white collar jobs anymore, and neither will blue collar jobs or any current version of a colored-collar job. The definition of a gray collar job (a hybrid of white and blue collar jobs) may have to change to reflect this transition toward technology management skillsets.

For the time being, let's refer to these future, tech-savvy versions of today's jobs as STEM "lite." STEM lite jobs will require most workers to know how to code. They also will need to know how to teach machines to learn skills and perform tasks, for instance, and manage digital and virtual resources. Maintenance specialists will work with smart infrastructure in virtual environments. Drones, AI and smart environments will assist police officers. Decision makers will be assisted by natural language AIs plugged into big data, big compute and big analytics solutions. Not everyone will be an IT professional, but everyone will be a technologist.

THE POTENTIAL GOLD MINE OF HUMAN-MACHINE PARTNERSHIPS

One of the questions we hear a lot these days is "will machines replace humans in the workplace?" Translation: "Will machines take my job away from me?" The answer isn't complicated, but it isn't simple either. Yes. No. Well... not exactly.

First, let's acknowledge reality. Technology disrupts markets. Industries rise and fall regularly, and so do job categories. You don't see a lot of chimney sweepers anymore, for instance, or street lamp lighters or traveling salesmen. When was the last time you met a livery attendant? Someday, when all cars are self driving and electric, we may look back on gas station attendants and taxi drivers in the same way. The path that business automation is on strongly suggests that machines soon will handle most repetitive, menial tasks. Call them bots, AI or digital assistants, it doesn't matter.
As computers and devices grow more intelligent and capable, their ability to autonomously manage your schedule, organize your day, pay your bills, order your food, book your flights, or reply to emails grows a little more every day. As our friend Jeremiah Owyang, founder of Crowd Companies, often reminds us, there isn't a single job that

won't someday be done by a machine. Accountant? Check. Customer service representative? Check. Recruiter or HR manager? Check. Math teacher? Check. Airline pilot? Check. Neurosurgeon? Check. Investment adviser? Check. Media planner? Check. CEO, COO and CFO? Check. But these examples don't mean that machines will take over all jobs. Just because machines could someday replace humans in every profession doesn't mean that will happen 10 years from now, 30 years from now or ever.

What is most likely to emerge instead is a human-machine partnership ecosystem. Think augmented capacity rather than outright replacement. Look at it this way: What makes more sense? Replacing a talented CEO with a genius-level AI, or assigning a genius-level AI to assist and advise that talented CEO? Here's another example. What makes more sense? Replacing a talented hiring manager/recruiter with a highly-specialized recruiting AI, or assigning a highly specialized recruiting AI to assist and advise that talented recruiter? See where we're going with this? What is ultimately more valuable to an organization? Replacing workers with machines, or augmenting the productivity and effectiveness of workers by helping them partner with machines to get more done?

Don't get us wrong; some jobs will disappear. Financial advisors, customer service representatives, accountants and bookkeepers, cashiers, truck drivers... there's going to be a good deal of contraction there. By virtue of making individual workers more productive by way of bots, digital assistants and helpful AI, organizations will likely, at least for a time, make adjustments to their workforce. But (there's always a but) new categories of jobs will emerge. HVAC specialists replaced chimney sweepers. Electrical engineers and maintenance workers replaced lamp lighters Traveling salesmen were, to some extent, replaced by mail-order catalog designers, who were in turn replaced by digital marketers. The wave of disruption coming at us now is no different. As job categories die, new ones will rise and replace them. Industrial robots need maintenance. Software needs developers. The IoT needs engineers. Even self-driving cars need oil changes.

One aspect of this human-machine partnership that we are particularly excited about is the inevitable commoditization of "bots" and digital assistants. It already takes only a few minutes to create a bot, or assign one to a task, inside of collaboration platforms like Cisco Spark or Slack. You don't need to know how to write code for this. You don't even need to be technically inclined or know what you're doing. You just follow the instructions and you're done. As accessible as this capability already is, it will only get easier and more pain free from here. By making bots, digital assistants and AI solutions technically and economically accessible to all, by eliminating barriers of entry, and by democratizing their use everyone has the opportunity to become more productive, versatile, efficient, and valuable to an employer or client. Ask yourself this, what couldn't you do or accomplish, armed with a team of digital assistants and handy AIs?

If, like us, part of your day includes doing research on a variety of technology- and business-related topics, a digital assistant can handle much of the research for you—organize it, summarize it and essentially function as a research assistant (or a team of research assistants) so you can focus on other tasks. If you're a sales manager, creating a team of digital assistants and AIs to handle your appointments, schedule your follow-ups, manage your team, and convert notes into reports can help you maximize your face time with customers, clients and prospects. If you're the CEO of a small company, and there obviously aren't enough hours in the day to put out every fire and get everything done, just imagine the things you could do with a small army of bots and digital assistants tasked with handling a hundred different tasks for you, all while analyzing data, alerting you to emerging opportunities, running financial projections and market simulations, and helping you make good decisions and, avoid bad ones.

This extends far beyond business, by the way. Machine-human partnerships can empower many seniors and people living with disabilities to avoid moving to assisted-living facilities, for instance. People living in remote areas, or with limited mobility, can better manage their own health, finances and personal safety with bots. A combination of sensors, drones, autonomous vehicles, robots, and AI can help farmers better manage their operations, minimize risks and maximize yields.

Human-machine partnerships will define the future of work for decades to come. Start planning for that change now.

CHAPTER 3:

CHANGE

The Proven Virtues of Adopting Operational Agility as a Model

"THE ONLY CONSTANT IS CHANGE." - TRANSFORMATION, ADAPTATION AND SURVIVAL IMPERATIVES

The only constant is change. Every day your industry, workforce and customers are changing a little. It isn't until we look back at a timeline that we usually see the change, milestone-by-milestone, quarter-by-quarter, year-by-year. In a sense, we are all like the proverbial frog being slowly boiled in a pot of water. The change in water temperature is so minute and imperceptible that we aren't able to see change in real time. Though we aren't literally being boiled to death, many companies are figuratively being boiled to death by change they fail to "feel," acknowledge or adapt to.

An important insight here is that just because you can't see or feel change doesn't mean it isn't happening. Change is always happening, one ticking second after another. Weather patterns affect shipping channels. Civil wars affect the price of commodities. Shifts in investments affect economic trajectories. Regulatory decisions affect the pace of innovation. Baby Boomer workers are retiring and being replaced by digital natives. Augmented reality is coming to our phones. Digital assistants and bots are coming to project management and business analysis. 3D-printing is coming to manufacturing. Virtual reality is coming to material and engineering design. Smart objects and smart environments are embedding themselves everywhere. Self-driving vehicles are coming, as is the end of fossil fuel dominance in energy markets. Change is happening all the time. Organizations and leaders who understand this, and operate with this in mind, tend to be better at managing, driving, shaping, and leveraging change as a strategy instead of seeing it as a problem or a necessary evil.

That's why change-averse leadership isn't leadership at all. True leaders are always looking for ways to change, improve and evolve. True leadership is always planning for change, hoping for it and investing in it. Evolution and adaptation don't happen overnight. They happen over time. Sometimes change comes abruptly and it may seem like it comes as a shock, but that is more a question of execution than one of preparation. Leaders always prepare for change, anticipate it and ready themselves for it so that, when an abrupt shift happens, it is less of a shock to the organization than it would have been had the shift come entirely without warning and the organization been utterly unprepared.

Watching for sea changes, threats and opportunities, trends, and signs of industry, economic, political, and technological change are as essential to futureproofing an organization, baking adaptability and operational agility into that organization's DNA.

CHANGE MANAGEMENT AND NEW PARADIGMS OF OPERATIONAL AGILITY AS A MODEL

If you aren't adapting, you're losing. It's as simple as that. Complacency is a silent killer. But, sometimes, adaptation and change don't come at you in the form of technology, processes, organizational behavior, or from any of the obvious places you would expect. Sometimes change turns up in the oddest places and even a little bit of it can pull the rug out from under you.

Consider the ripple effects of change for a moment. What is commonly known as "the Butterfly Effect." The Butterfly Effect is a theory used to show that one small change somewhere can create a chain reaction of increasingly larger changes that can be felt around the world. Thus, a butterfly beating its wings in Caracas might, through a series of ripples of cause and effect, contribute to a major typhoon in the Philippines. The notion is as hyperbolic as it is poetic, but it does hold some measure of truth. Actions cause reactions, and those reactions in turn cause more reactions, and so on. In business, the proverbial butterfly usually manifests itself as a big idea, and, as we all know, one revolutionary idea can completely disrupt an industry. Examples of these types of ideas include touch screens, paper cups, USB drives, wireless data transfers, self-driving cars, magnetic strips, cloud computing, and solar panels. Each one of these ideas drives change. Upon their creation, companies suddenly need new tools, skills, processes and methodologies, facilities, taxonomies, departments, competencies, quality control standards, licensing language, and even new metrics.

How do you adapt traditional industry success metrics like market share and market penetration when your company is in the process of disrupting an industry? How do you communicate success, progress and potential to investors when you are in the process of creating a new product or industry category? We saw companies struggle with new metrics when social media began to insert itself into the business world. Social media gurus advocated the end of traditional ROI (return on investment) and recommended instead that companies measure likes and followers as a measure of success, or that ROI shift to return on all sorts of things, from relationships to inspiration. Some companies probably still struggle with social media measurement, which is to say that they still struggle with change, even after a decade of Facebook and Twitter business integration.

Change is as much about problem solving as it is anything else. Change management isn't about process adoption, it's about figuring out how to make things that don't work as well as they should work better. When you change something, it isn't going to work the way it once did. Change is going to create some problems, even if it brings a considerable improvement to a task or function, like a faster computing time, better video quality, a more comfortable flight, or bigger reach for a piece of content. Some of these problems will be expected, others will not. Those kinks have to be ironed out. You have to make adjustments. You have to adapt. That process of adaptation is what we call change management, and, yes, it's a process.

Because change management is a process, it requires a certain degree of specialization and competence. Change management is a function, a role. It isn't a haphazard do-it-yourself scheme. Companies that weather change well don't usually do so by letting their employees figure things out on their own. Most companies tried that with social media measurement, and we all know how well that turned out. The same is true of any kind of change. For example, a company's workforce transitioning from Boomers to millennials in a short span of time, retooling for 100 percent electric car production by 2025, transitioning from being a hardware company to a Cloud services company, actively promoting diversity across all departments, replacing all desktop computers with laptops, tablets, and smartphones; introducing gamification as a means of developing and motivating employees, or shifting from a focus on products and services to a focus on experiences. It isn't enough to come up with the idea and sign off on it. Someone has to implement the idea and manage its execution from design to deployment. Someone also has to be there to make sure all of the seams are in the right places and that they will hold.

Manufacturing engineers tend to be pretty adept at this. They understand how objects fit in space. They know how much square footage they'll need to install a new machine, how much power it will need to run, what kind of training its operators will need, how plant logistics will have to be adapted to the change, what spare parts they'll need in case it breaks down, and so on. Change management is hard, detailed work that never wants for minutiae. If it takes a team of manufacturing engineers to manage change in a plant environment, it means that you need a white-collar team with similar skills to pull it off in an office environment. Companies that invest in change management expertise tend to fare much better than companies that don't.

Change management expertise doesn't have to be 100 percent in house. Most companies rely on consultants, change management experts, corporate trainers, and other contract-based experts to help them transition from *before* to *after*. But, when change is a constant and increasingly an operational imperative, it stands to reason that change management should be brought in-house. Cultural nuances and internal politics, the minefields of most large organizations, often escape outside experts. Managing change is as much about knowing the terrain as it is about translating best practices into actionable methodologies.

Speaking of best practices, forget everything you think you know about them. Instead, study what works for other companies, adapt what you can to your own, keep what works, and either fix what doesn't or get rid of it. There are few effective cookie-cutter best practices. Everything has to be tweaked and adjusted. Everything has to be painstakingly customized to work properly. Universal change management best practices are a myth. What works for Land Rover won't work for Ford. What works for Air France won't work for United Airlines. Internal cultures are unique. Internal subcultures within those cultures are unique as well. Outsourced change management can only do so much. For change management to work, the people in charge of it must have intimate knowledge of the ins and outs of the companies, groups, departments, and teams they will work with or they will fail. The lesson here is this: Companies that invest in change management expertise and deploy it across their organizations, then work toward creating a culture of operational agility, are far more futureproof than organizations that don't invest in change management expertise, don't deploy change management expertise across their organizations, and don't create and foster cultures of operational agility.

Companies that know how to retool and reorganize quickly in times of disruption win. This ability to adjust takes focus, discipline and diligence.

To illustrate how pretty much any company, no matter how old or traditionally "non-digital," can embrace change and turn itself into a digital business, look no further than Burberry. Unlike many of the companies in this book, the upscale London-based fashion brand is old.

Way old. Burberry was established in 1856.

At its heart though, Burberry was always an innovative business. Thomas Burberry, the founder, wasn't a fan of the era's rubberized Mackintosh raincoats, so he set out to make a better all-weather garment. He designed a breathable waterproof fabric, trademarked the term "gabardine," and set out to disrupt the garment industry with his invention and branding savvy. Burberry raincoats were battle-tested during the first world war, and dubbed "trench coats" after acquitting themselves well in the trenches of France and Flanders. The brand's famous Burberry Check pattern was initially a lining for the trench coats, but, after the war, Burberry started making it more conspicuous. On a whim, an enterprising Burberry store owner in Paris ordered a few umbrellas in the check pattern for a runway show, and they were so successful that the store turned the accessory into a genuine product. Its success led to the creation of the Burberry Check scarf, which, through its immediate and continued success, propelled the brand even further.

So far, we haven't talked about digital transformation, but we wanted to make the point that Burberry was always, on some level, a company whose fortunes were tied to experimentation and innovation. Most successful companies are, even if they sometimes forget and lose their way for a little while.

Fast forward to 2006, Burberry was struggling to remain relevant. Generations of customers had come and gone, and the brand was falling behind the times. That was when Adriana Ahrendts, Burberry's CEO, decided to shake things up and get the company back on track. Rather than bolting digital onto the brand's marketing, like most other fashion brands were doing at the time, Ahrendts saw the sea change brought about by technology, understood the need to transform rather than just pivot, and went all in. She wanted to remake Burberry into the first digital-first fashion brand, which, she rightly surmised, was the best way to reach new generations of shoppers. Between 2006 and 2014, that is exactly what Burberry set out to do.

Social media was one of the company's first areas of focus and where it firmly planted its flag. The approach was clever. It didn't require the company to rebuild its IT infrastructure or make expensive and risky technology plays. Social combined media and tech in a way that was challenging enough, but not overly daunting or impossible to tackle. In addition to building a strong and active presence on social media channels, Burberry created themed microsites for campaigns, like The Art of the Trench, where customers could post photos wearing their own trench coats. In 2010, it streamed its spring/summer fashion show live, which was a bold and innovative idea back then. By 2011, Burberry's Facebook page boasted over a million followers – more than any other fashion brand at the time.

More importantly, Burberry started noticing a boost in sales: Roughly 50 percent growth YoY. Putting digital at the center of the Burberry brand was already paying off.

Burberry also completely revamped its web presence. Burberry. com was designed to create a clean, aspirational, authentic digital experience, and make shopping easy, regardless of device or browser. Seamless digital experiences were at the core of every decision that went into the design of the company's site—a strategy still not adopted by the majority of traditional retail-driven companies adjusting to the new rules of the digital space. Burberry also introduced product customization capabilities to its digital shopping properties to combine its bespoke image and the utility of digital shopping technologies. Customers now are able to easily customize their products and make them uniquely their own, which drives sales, brand affinity and loyalty.

In terms of digital technology integration, Burberry also pushed the envelope of brick and mortar retail experiences. The company's flagship store in London was redesigned to act as a physical manifestation of the company's digital first strategy. It boasts hundreds of digital displays and speakers to create a lush and unique shopping experience. But the changes aren't merely cosmetic. They are also brilliantly functional. Using RFID chips on certain products and pairing their frequency to proximity sensors, the store's displays, especially around the fitting rooms, customize their content to match nearby shopper's current choices, thereby softly validating their purchase intent.

Even before Burberry had fully realized its own digital transformation potential, it went from a slow downward trajectory to becoming the fourth fastest growing brand in the world in just under five years. Stretched across a 10-year timeframe, Burberry's comeback is even more impressive. Its annual revenue of roughly £750 million in 2006 grew to more than £2.5 billion in 2016. How did Burberry, a traditional fashion house founded before the U.S. Civil War, manage to turn itself into a market juggernaut in just under 10 years? By embracing digital transformation and reinventing itself as a digital first company.

BANKING: CRYPTOCURRENCIES, DIGITAL WALLETS AND THE REINVENTION OF FINANCIAL SERVICES

Think about the growth of mobile payments in the last few years, for instance, and how transformative that shift has been. Frictionless payments have become the new Holy Grail of retail and banking experiences, right? (Aside from achieving reliable cybersecurity, but that is a topic for a different day.) Think about the trend toward frictionless transaction.

We started with cash. Cash in wallets, that had to be fished out of a pocket or a purse, then folded open. Cash then had to be plucked out, counted, handed over, recounted, sorted, slipped into a till, the transaction recorded by manual button-pushing, and then change counted, returned, recounted, and stored away. Maximum friction.

Then came checks. Checks in checkbooks that had to be fished out of a pocket or a purse, then folded open. A pen had to be produced, then the amount entered in letters and numbers, names and signatures applied, then the check had to be carefully torn free and handed over with an ID. A few manual operations later, the check was slipped into the till, the transaction manually entered into it, and the checkbook and ID had to be put back in their pockets or purses. Still maximum friction. (And if you haven't been in line behind someone writing a check recently, consider yourself lucky.)

Then came credit cards: Produce wallet. Produce card. Hand over card. Place card in machine. Carefully slide form and carbon paper into machine. Operate the moving part of the machine to create an imprint of the card on the form. Enter the transaction in the till. Hand the card back to the customer, tear off receipts… Still lots of friction.

Then came credit card readers, where you have to get our your wallet, produce your card, slide or insert your card into the card reader, type in a code, and approve the amount. If you're lucky, you then can put your card back in your wallet. If you aren't, you have to sign a receipt, then put your card back in your wallet. Still, this process contains significantly less friction than before. Here, we begin to see improvement

Then came mobile payments. With this type of payment, you can swipe your phone over a sensor and approve the transaction with a tap or a swipe of the finger, or just handle the entire transaction from inside a phone app. There is virtually no friction.

What's next? Frictionless transactions. Once a customer is identified by a combination of digital handshakes and sensors, he or she can fill up a shopping cart or shopping bag and leave the store without having to wait for a cashier to scan every individual item and without having to effectuate a credit card transaction. The entire process is automated and runs in the background. To a time-traveling observer from the Y2K era, it would look as if shoppers no longer needed to pay for anything because the act of paying itself will be handled automatically by smart devices and software.

Amazon and Walmart are experimenting with frictionless payment systems for brick-and-mortar retail environments, and, as this book goes to print, are about to deploy the model in several retail locations around the U.S. Walmart's program is called "Scan & Go," and it allows shoppers to scan the products they purchase as they add them to their carts, either with their phone or a store-supplied scanner, and pay for them without going through a traditional checkout. The program already is being rolled out in Texas, Georgia, Florida, and Kentucky. Amazon's program called "Amazon Go" appears to be even more frictionless as it makes use of sensors and machine learning to automatically identify items being added to a shopping cart (no manual scanning required). Like Walmart's system, checkout is virtual.

Aside from the net benefit of understanding where retail payments and customer experiences are headed (and all businesses with physical, brick-and-mortar checkouts should pay attention, from retailers to hotels and hospitals), there is a broader lesson here about following trends to their logical next evolutions. The evolution of the retail payment experience has, for decades, driven itself toward frictionless payment experiences that are faster, painless and secure. A metaphorical evolution from long lines to short lines to no lines. Taking a step back, it isn't hard to see what trajectory retail payment experiences were on all along. The same principle can be applied to just about any trend. The trick is to take the time to take that step back and look at the evolution of technologies, consumer trends and business trends from a different perspective. Not a 10,000-foot view, as the expression goes, but rather from a historical perspective. (Borrowing the above analogy, about 500 feet will do.)

For instance, what can we conclude about the trajectory of automobiles in the United States? Are we moving, in the long term, toward big, gasoline-guzzling SUVs or toward energy-efficient electric vehicles of all shapes and sizes? What conclusions can we draw about public transportation in Europe? What can we surmise about IoT integration into urban areas and the potential for smart cities? Take a step back. Start from the beginning. Plot the trajectory so far. Find the common thread. Our examples above point to three trajectories—nergy efficiency, the elimination of traffic congestion and pollution in cities, and smart, connected and self-managing infrastructure.

Now focus your newly-acquired 500-foot trendspotting skill to healthcare, banking, finance, entertainment, news, manufacturing, aerospace, tourism, travel, the white collar workplace, mobility, or agriculture. Take a step back. Start from the beginning. Plot the trajectory so far. Find the common thread. What do you see? If you want to futureproof your business, one of the most effective skills you can develop is the ability to determine where things appear to be going and steer your organization toward that.

If you're a healthcare provider, you may want to start looking into the democratization of health management and telemedicine. If you're in finance and banking, you should be looking into blockchain, machine learning and how AI can help you build the next generation of investment advisor services. If you're in agriculture, you should be looking into sensor technologies, smart drones, the IoT, and predictive analytics. If you're in tourism and entertainment, you should be looking carefully into mixed reality technologies (like augmented reality and virtual reality) and real-time language processing solutions.

More than anything, organizations need to be able to take that same step back and make sure their trajectory is in line. Strategies and business plans that seemed on target three years ago may be completely out of date already. Focus points and initiatives that made sense six months ago may have seized on short-term trends, but missed the larger ones. Pushing forward with a strategic vision that is already obsolete could be disastrous, so it is vital for organizations to continually assess industry trends and simultaneously assess whether their own trajectories are in line with those trends.

ENGINEERING THE END OF RESISTANCE

We spend a good deal of time talking about data-driven decision making in this book. That's because resistance to change is usually its biggest obstacle. Complacency, an inadequate change management infrastructure, uninspired leadership, a lack of vision, a disengaged workforce, or fear of failure, discomfort or the unknown… these obstacles are among the many that can stand in the way of change. But, when it comes down to brass tack, it's resistance from people in your organization that gets in the way of progress.

In entrenched siloed organization, you have your fiefdoms and their turf wars. They are the "I don't answer to you" managers and the "I'll nod like I agree, but I'm not changing the way I do things" luddites. People will resist change out of principle, for no other reason than they can, and it gives them a sense of power and influence over their little corners of the office. In less siloed organizations, resistance usually comes in the form of fear or reluctance because of questions like:

- Will this change make my life more difficult?

- Will this change mean a lot more work?

- Will this change make it harder for me to hit my targets and make my bonus?

- Will this change make me have to work longer hours?

- Will this change make me lose hours?

- Will this change make my job obsolete?

- Will this change kill my chances at a promotion?

- Will this change force me to move to another part of the country?

- Will this change put me on a new team with a bunch of strangers?

- Will this change force me to have to relearn everything?

Fight or flight -> Change equals unknown -> Unknown equals threat -> Threat equals fear -> Fear triggers fight or flight reflex.

Fight manifests itself as active resistance, pushing back. This often comes in the form of explaining why the proposed change won't work, why it's a bad idea, why it's the wrong time for it, why it can't be done, why it will cause more problems than it aims to solve. Fight is "you can't make me." Fight is "no thank you. Try again next year maybe."

Flight manifests itself as escape. This may include prioritizing everything relating to the change or finding excuses about why it isn't operationally feasible. Flight is "we don't have the budget." Flight is "we don't have the bandwidth." Flight is "we don't have the resources." Flight is "even if we could, we probably need to put this off until later, when we're better equipped to do this."

If fight and flight are products of fear, then you have to remove fear from the equation. Simple.

How do you do make people less afraid of change (or not afraid of it at all)? You make change less scary. How do you do that? You turn questions into answers. You turn unknown quantities into known quantities. You show people in your org the payoff of that change, not in terms of hypotheticals, but in terms of concrete, measurable, crystal-clear outcomes.

- **Will this change make my life more difficult?**

For about three weeks, maybe a little. After that, no. It will make your life much easier. Here's how...

- **Will this change mean a lot more work?**

No. It will mean just a little more work for a few weeks, but no more than maybe 30 minutes a day at the most. After that, you will spend a lot less time on this kind of task, actually. Here's a graph of the before and after.

- **Will this change make it harder for me to hit my targets and make my bonus?**

No. It will make it easier for you to hit your targets and make your bonus. That's why we're implementing this change. The whole point is to help you be more successful, not less. Let me show you how.

- **Will this change make me have to work longer hours?**

No. We've looked at that, and your hours won't change.

- **Will this change make me lose hours?**

No. We've made it so your schedule won't change because of this.

- **Will this change make my job obsolete?**

No. We have no plans to automate or outsource your job. But, if you're afraid of that happening at some point in the future, we have training programs that you might want to look into that will give you more career flexibility. Here are some resources.

- **Will this change kill my chances at a promotion?**

No. This change, like all changes we make around here, are intended to improve outcomes. If anything, this change may help you get a promotion if you use it to your advantage. Let me show you.

- **Will this change force me to move to another part of the country?**

  (Maybe. That happens.) If not, then no. It isn't that kind of change. Let's look at what we're talking about.

- **Will this change put me on a new team with a bunch of strangers?**

  If not, no. If yes, a new team environment will help you grow, acquire new skills and open up more opportunities for you. We will help you be successful. We think you'll be a perfect fit, though. You're perfect for it. Let me show you what we mean.

- **Will this change force me to have to relearn everything?**

  No, not everything. You'll only need to relearn a few new things. We don't want to invalidate what you're already good at. We want to build on it. It's a great opportunity to train up and help us be more competitive. Let me show you.

These are simple conversations that don't take a lot of time to have but that need to happen. Fear of the unknown is easily remedied when you turn the unknown into the known. Use data and data modeling to show people how change will help them rather than impede of threaten them. Invite their questions and doubts, then answer and address them. Recognize that, if employees ask a question about a change you hope to implement, but you don't have an answer for it, you've come to the negotiating table unprepared.

And yes, we said "negotiating table" because, ultimately, that's what it is. Regardless of your authority, you are negotiating terms with your employees when you change the way they work. You're asking them to put their faith in you and take a risk with you. In return, you have to answer their questions. You need to provide them with assurances that you have done your homework, that you have anticipated every problem and ripple, and that you haven't rushed into a decision you didn't completely understand.

You can't fight resistance with force or authority. You have to fight it by cutting it off from what fuels it. Data-driven decision making is one of the most effective ways of doing that. Whether you're using an advanced cognitive computing tool like IBM's Watson to do predictive analysis, or a virtualization tool like Dassault Systèmes' 3DExcite to create virtual models of what you are trying to create, or another data analytics and modeling solution doesn't really matter as long as you use tools that will help you model and test the change you want to enact in your organization before committing to that change. Companies didn't have these tools 20 years ago. At best, you had an Excel spreadsheet and a whiteboard to show employees how reshuffling an assembly line could save the company millions of dollars per year and keep manufacturing from moving overseas. We have sat in conference rooms where change was shown as dots on a map and numbers on a whiteboard changing from red to green. The process isn't new. The tools are just getting better.

Now we're seeing change explained with hands-on demonstrations of augmented reality capabilities in manufacturing, retail, healthcare, and office environments. We see change tested and modeled in real time by analytics tools that an entire team can play around with on their portable devices. The same analytics software that can map a stock portfolio's performance over time can be used to model the impact of a workplace change on income projections, deltas in work hours, employee productivity, and employee engagement. Convincing employees that change is good isn't that hard if you or someone working for you has made sure that the changes you want to make will result in the outcomes you hope for.

Bonus: Not only does eliminating resistance to change make your organization more agile and adaptable, it accelerates the velocity of that change. What might have taken your company six months to do might take three if you can get everyone on the same page right from the start. Think about the impact that can have on your competitiveness, your reputation in your industry and your ability to be a first mover when the opportunity next presents itself.

We won't pretend that people will always be reasonable. Some people will refuse to change, bend or budge, no matter how well you make your case. As unfortunate as it is, they may just have to go. Sometimes to move forward you have to let go of the past, or at least the parts of it that will only weigh you down and impede your progress. It's painful and difficult, but no company can afford to have people who try to paddle backward while everything depends on paddling quickly forward. If members of your organization don't want to be part of your journey of transformation, perhaps it's time for them to find a company that is more aligned with their professional world view.

ENGINEERING THE END OF SILOS

During the Middle Ages, lords and kings built castles with walls and towers to protect what was theirs and to project authority. The bigger the castle, the more it projected over their fiefdoms.

Organizational silos are the corporate versions of this antiquated, obsolete mentality that kept people apart and ideas from spreading for hundreds of years. Organizational silos are nothing but walled fiefdoms. Even the roles they perpetuate are the same. You have your lords, your gatekeepers, your treasurers, your internal politics and palace intrigue, your laborers and serfs, your rules, and even your skirmishes with other lords and their fiefdoms.

Silos are absurd and counterproductive, and, for decades now, they have been slowly killing companies that allow them to exist. To survive the next decade, companies that still allow silos have to break them down and get rid of them once and for all.

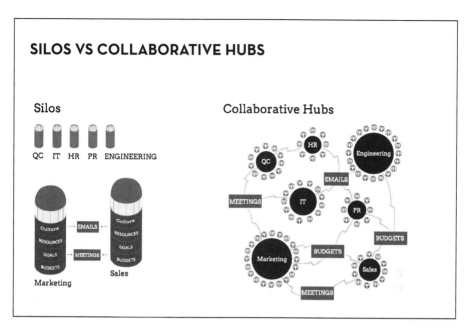

flat vs silos.

This is one of those topics where we don't want to walk a fine line. On our best day, we will make an effort to be diplomatic about this and explain that, rather than eliminate silos altogether, companies can start by building bridges between them. Establish and grow connective tissue, we would suggest. Ease your organization into the change. Let the silos die slow deaths brought on by a thousand small acts of collaboration. It's good advice, but, for many organizations, it might not be enough. There is no time to waste, and we caution that accommodating laggards, contrarian, and department managers who are in no way interested in helping you futureproof your company is nothing more than a waste of time.

Here's a simple rule of futureproofing: If someone insists on becoming an obstacle, treat them like one. Push them out of the way and keep going. If you need your organization to go in one direction, and some of your managers or executives are rowing away from your goal, they aren't on your side. They aren't interested in the future. All they are doing is getting in the way. Get rid of them.

In organizations, silos aren't real. There aren't physical walls, ramparts or gates. Silos are social constructs designed to hoard resources like budgets, talent, equipment, office space, and man hours. That isn't how successful companies operate anymore. Not when IT has to embed itself into every business function. Not when market intelligence, data and analysis have to be able to flow freely from one corner of the organization to another. Not when problem-solving, innovation and digital transformation cannot occur at scale without deep and fluid collaboration across the entire company.

Kill your silos or they will kill you. It's that simple. Make this a priority immediately.

SLOW IS SMOOTH; SMOOTH IS FAST. - ESTABLISHING BEST PRACTICES FOR CHANGE MANAGEMENT

There's an expression you're likely to run into in the special forces community: "Slow is smooth; smooth is fast." It refers to movement and muscle memory. It applies to pretty much everything, from how a team moves together to how an operator draws and fires his weapon. The advice emphasizes good form: Whatever you're doing, better to do it right than to rush it and screw it up. A bullet is worthless if it's off target, and it doesn't matter how fast you're moving if the enemy sees you coming. Good advice if you're a soldier, but there's value to that advice in the business world also, particularly as it relates to digital transformation and futureproofing, where some of the same concepts apply.

There is a balance to be struck between moving too slow and too fast, especially when working on new skills, building a new business model or transforming an organization. You know that you want to be fast, fluid and effective at some point. Whether you're looking for your company to be able to adapt to change in record time, or you want to be able to jump on new market opportunities as they emerge, you have to understand this is a process that takes time. It may take months or even years, and that's alright. The way you get there is by working the basics—breaking things down one skillset at a time, one competency at a time—and through repetition, experimentation and patience, taking the time to become supremely good at them all. As your organization's fluency improves, you start building on the basics by combining skillsets and capabilities. Instead of breaking things down, you start assembling them into high-level functions. In most organizations, that looks like cross-functional working groups or the sort of silo-free, organic, real-time collaboration that we talked about in the book already.

Slow is smooth; smooth is fast. A well-oiled machine may not look fast, but it's efficient. It doesn't get excited. It doesn't lose its calm. It doesn't stumble. It knows what to do because it has rehearsed it and done it a million times, because it does all that is necessary to succeed.

All day, every day:

- Digital transformation

- Collaboration

- Gamification

- Continuous improvement

- Solving problems for one another

- Creating amazing experiences for everyone

- Integrating new digital tools into everyday tasks

- Learning how to do things better and smarter

Change is hard, but it's necessary. And, at the current pace of change, it is supremely difficult for most organizations to keep up. It's easy to fall behind because of caution, and it's also easy to rush in the wrong direction or to get sloppy by moving too fast in an effort to catch up. We find that more often than not, it's unusual little insights like this that can make all the difference. Slow is smooth; smooth is fast is the sort of thing you are far more likely to learn on a gun range than in an MBA program, and that's too bad because it is probably one of the most critical bits of advice you will receive relative to change management. Whatever you do, if you and your employees focus on learning the business equivalent of proper form and technique, you will build a culture of not only fluid competence but confidence in change. You will build an organization that trusts in the process of transformation. Businesses that are able to do that are one step closer to knowing how to become future proof.

Take Nike, for instance. Nike is the world's undisputed dominant brand in athletic apparel, footwear, equipment, accessories, and services. While the company is relatively young (it was founded in 1964 by Phil Knight and Bill Bowerman as "Blue Ribbon Sports"), the Oregon-based company has been a market juggernaut since it rebranded itself as "Nike" in 1971. It now boasts an impressive $30 billion in annual revenue from sales spanning the globe, and, while other global brands like Adidas and Under Armour have worked for every ounce of market share they can claim for themselves, Nike is the incumbent brand in its space. But remaining supreme in an industry isn't easy. You have to adapt to change, and Nike is no different.

The first major milestone in Nike's digital transformation came in 1999 when the company started using the web to sell products directly to its customers. This marked a big shift. For the first time in its history, Nike didn't have to depend on retailers to drive sales.

Bonus impact: Not only did Nike now have the ability to sell and ship directly to consumers, it also had the ability to engage with customers via the web, collect demographic and behavioral data, and begin to better understand not only their overall customer segments, but the subcategories of customers that made up the ecosystem of athletic subcultures that Nike now taps into. By subcultures, we mean the different tribes of athletes that make up general sports categories. Recreational 5K runners don't have the same needs as long-distance trail runners, for instance. They speak a different language, have different concerns, and look to augment their shoe purchases with different types of accessories. The content they look for is different as well. Athletic subcultures are athletic tribes, and tribes have their own language, needs, and expectations, and require their own spaces in the Nike universe. In 1999, things weren't yet as clear as they are now, but selling directly to consumers opened the door to an enormous opportunity for Nike— one no longer limited by retail space, retail specialization, and the types of physical constraints that had kept Nike from penetrating hundreds of passionate and underserved athletic communities.

Digital transformation milestone No. 2: In 2006, Nike entered the world of activity tracking and wearable fitness sensors with the launch of the Nike+ iPod kit, which allowed runners to connect a piezoelectric sensor (attached to a running shoe) to an iPod. In 2008, this capability was enhanced by the release of Apple's iPod Touch, which linked directly to the sensor's Nike+ signals. These capabilities improved and grew with every successive iteration of the iPhone, with established heart rate monitor brand Polar jumping into the mix to sweeten the deal for serious runners.

The FuelBand was introduced in 2012. Although the launch, which targeted recreational athletes and sedentary consumers looking for new ways to stay motivated during their fitness journeys, boosted sales in Nike's Equipment division by 18 percent, the product received mixed reviews. On the positive side, the data tracking and gamification aspects of the product were clever. Users uploaded their data by way of the Nike+ Connect portal, and posted it to their Nike+ web-based profile to track their progress, earn rewards and share their stats with their Facebook friends. We like gamification, and we've seen it work rather well with other digital athletic communities like Strava and Garmin Connect, so the FuelBand was smart. It drove sales of a Nike product, increased daily exposure to the brand, helped build community-based bonds around the brand and athletic activity, helped form habits that would presumably help drive sales and positive word-of-mouth, and positioned Nike as a leader in the fitness tracker/wearable space. The flip side of that is FuelBand was perhaps too basic a fitness tracker for serious athletes who expected the degree of functionality already offered by companies like Garmin and Suunto. FuelBand also was criticized for being one of the least accurate fitness trackers on the market, in some cases less accurate than a smartphone[5], which did nothing to improve the tracker's value proposition. By 2014, negative feedback had killed FuelBand, and the project was scrapped.

Nike learned from this failure, however, and went back to the drawing board. FuelBand had failed, but the Nike+ concept hadn't. Connectivity across devices and Nike products was a win. The online community model was a win. Fitness tracking, data analysis, gamification, and

---

5 Johnston, Chris. «Fitness Bands 'less Accurate than Smartphones' in Counting Steps.» *The Guardian.* Guardian News and Media, 11 Feb. 2015. Web. 02 Mar. 2017.

the digitization of athletic performance was a win. Not just a win, but a largely untapped opportunity for a global brand like Nike. The trick to making it work was that Nike needed to start thinking less like a product company and more like a platform company.

In 2014, the platform model was beginning to prove its potential. Google, Apple, Facebook, and Amazon, had leveraged the platform model to achieve success that Nike wanted to adapt to its own ecosystem. It was around that time that Nike started to look into ways of transitioning from being mostly a products and services company to being a platform company. If a single keyword can define the first phase of that evolution, it's integration. Following Apple's example, Nike worked to integrate all of its applications in the cloud so they would speak to each other with as little friction as possible. The general idea was to create an experience of fluid interaction, access to data, and feedback for consumers to allow them to better define and more easily achieve their health goals.[6]

How was this all achieved?
First, by identifying the opportunity. Second, by understanding the role that technology had to play in the company's ability to adapt and change. Third, by empowering someone in the organization to do something about it.

That third point is important, and Nike's success wouldn't be possible without it. Having a competent, driven, focused chief digital officer with a clear mandate was vital to the success of its digital transformation strategy. In 2016, Adam Sussman was named chief digital officer at Nike, marking it as the year Nike decided to finally get serious about its previously "long-runway" style digital transformation.

Note that the transition from product thinking (hardware) to platform thinking (software and new interwoven business models involving digital technologies) made it necessary for Nike to stop thinking about digital transformation as an abstract IT-related modernization of its business. Nike took its first real step toward becoming a platform company and taking digital transformation seriously when it created that CDO role. As an organization, it finally understood that only a C-level role could successfully drive

---

[6] How Nike Is Shifting to a Platform Business.» *Fortune*. Fortune, n.d. Web.

that vital an endeavor. It took perhaps longer for Nike to come to this realization than we would have hoped, but what matters is that Nike got there.

Now let's briefly talk about the role that leadership plays in empowerment and digital transformation at Nike. Mark Parker, Nike's CEO, is a fan of breakthroughs and innovation. He understands that Nike can't be Nike without being in the arena and taking chances. It isn't enough for Nike to exist. Nike has to win, which means that Nike has to drive the pace and push past its competitors. Internally, his leadership style manifests itself as a penchant for asking tough questions, but with an aim toward strategic discovery and empowerment. It's a little unusual, so let's allow Andy Campion, Nike's chief financial officer, to explain:

"What's fascinating about [Parker's] use of questions is that it leaves other leaders empowered to find the answers themselves and act on them."[7]

Per Mark Parker:
"I end up asking a lot of questions, so the team thinks things through. I don't say 'Do this, do that.' I'm not a micromanager. I don't believe in that. ...At Nike, we have incredibly strong people. They know what to do."[8]

If you look at leaders in terms of being diminishers or multipliers, it's easy to see how Parker's leadership style makes him an effective multiplier. Without an innovation-driven multiplier CEO like Mark Parker, it's unlikely that the CDO role would exist at Nike today or that it would be empowered to deliver truly transformative results.

Since buy-in is also crucial to digital transformation, it's important for companies to create more momentum and support for digital transformation initiatives than just a mandate from the CEO to the CDO. Other senior executives and board members have to be on the same page. For Nike, one of those executives is Trevor Edwards, president of Nike brand. Edwards was instrumental in the development of Nike+ and saw early on the value of connecting all

[7]Lebowitz, Shana. «Here's the Leadership Strategy Nike's CEO Uses to Make Employees Smarter.» *Business Insider*. Business Insider, 14 Nov. 2015. Web. 02 Mar. 2017.
[8]Lebowitz, Shana. «Here's the Leadership Strategy Nike's CEO Uses to Make Employees Smarter.» *Business Insider*. Business Insider, 14 Nov. 2015. Web. 02 Mar. 2017.

of Nike's digital platforms and services, including amplifying Nike's presence in the social space.[9] It isn't difficult to see how a proven leader like Edwards finds himself in a unique position to support Sussman's digital transformation efforts, particularly as they pertain to Nike's transition to a platform model.

What we see here is a combination of factors leading to Nike's slow but steady transition to a digital business: A culture of innovation and experimentation, technology integration through strategic partnerships, a shift in mindset marked by a serious commitment to digital transformation, and a leadership culture transitioning to a focus on technology and disruptive innovation. Nike's steady and measured evolution reminds us of thousands of incumbent brands and businesses that may not have been the fastest to adapt to what is coming, but finally crossed that bridge and are now in an ideal position to remake themselves into the industry leaders for which the next three decades will be enormously rewarding.

[9] «Executives.» *About Nike - Executives*. Nike, n.d. Web. 02 Mar. 2017.

CHAPTER 4:

INNOVATION

How Companies that Learn to Fail Faster Tend to Engineer Big Wins

DREAMERS, PIONEERS, WIZARDS, AND TINKERERS: NO-SIZE-FITS-ALL INNOVATION

Innovation comes in all shapes and sizes. Apple reinvented the personal computer, the portable music player and the smartphone. Starbucks made drinking coffee out of an enormous white and green cup cool and special. Tesla brought us as close to affordable no-emissions sports cars as we could hope to get this soon in the 21st century. Amazon brought us voice-activated shopping from home. Qualcomm to this day continues to develop the technologies that make modern wireless communications possible and are bringing edge computing to the IoT. Dassault Systèmes is bringing 3D modeling to the masses. Oculus and Meta are making our VR and AR dreams a reality. The complete list of the world's innovators goes on forever. Someone had to invent the soda can tab. Someone had to invent that swivel your desk chair uses to angle your spine just right. Someone invented the process that makes your laptop know when to power down. Toasters, power outlets, pencil sharpeners, battery packs, zippers, razor blades, Bluetooth, energy-efficient light bulbs, laundry detergent, sun umbrellas... someone invented everything you buy .Everything around us, at one point or another, was an innovation. You don't have to be Steve Jobs, Bill Gates or Mark Zuckerberg to be an innovator or a pioneer, and you don't have to be a tech startup to build a successful culture of innovation. Any company can do it. If you can dream it, you can build it. And, if you can't, you can hire someone who will.

Look, we love innovation. Who doesn't? Innovation is a manifestation of genius. It's problem solving at its best. From the moment the first ancestor of mankind built the first spear, innovation was destined for greatness. Think about ancient ship builders, the first windmills or the first inventor who built a working pocket watch. Innovation is nothing short of miraculous. From poets, painters and writers to design engineers, chemical engineers and software engineers, innovation is one of the things that propels humanity forward. Innovation is what brought us out of caves and sent us into space. It's the reason you probably won't die of polio, the reason you can eat tomatoes all year and the reason the world of business is as exciting as ever. But innovation is also what will either make or break your business in the next five years.

If you blow off innovation (inside *and* outside your company), you're going to be left behind. If you incorporate it into your business, pursue it and invest in it properly, you might be okay. The future is built by innovation. It's always been the case, and the pace of innovation certainly hasn't slowed down in recent years. So if you aren't focusing on innovation, if you aren't prioritizing it, you aren't futureproofing your business. It's that simple.

Easier said than done though, right? Where does innovation come from? Engineers? Designers? Scientists? Dreamers? The answer is yes. It also comes from just observing the world around you, paying attention to what works and what doesn't, then figuring out ways of doing things better, faster or cheaper. Why did Ford invent the modern production line in 1913? Because 12 hours seemed like an awful long time to build just one car, and he had a lot of cars to build.

There's more to that legend, by the way. Ford didn't really invent the modern assembly line. Not in the sense that he invented the concept. He took a process of mass manufacturing, standardized parts and assembly that already had been developed in the late 1700s and early 1800s by inventors like Eli Whitney and Thomas Blanchard (no relation), then improved by others for more than a century, and he adapted it to his specific needs.

That too is innovation—building something new out of the ideas of others. Apple didn't invent the smartphone, for instance. Apple *reinvented* the smartphone. Many of the technical innovations that went into the first iPhone weren't even designed by Apple. Apple integrated the technology into their product though, and pushed the envelope of industrial design and user experience to make it all work smoothly. In doing so, Apple created something revolutionary and unique, something as transformative as Ford's assembly line almost a century before. Innovation, more often than not, is just improvement. You don't have to be a mad scientist locked up in a lab to invent the next big thing. More often than not, all you have to do is look at something you care about, something that could be improved, and then just improve it. If you can't do it yourself, you find someone who can. At its core, it's as simple as that. Every startup in the world is built on that simple premise.

We don't want to tell anyone to think more like a startup. It's cliché, overdone and you've already heard it a hundred times, if not a thousand... but you kind of have to start thinking like a startup, if only in relation to this one point— innovation *is* an act of will. For all the mystique around the role that genius plays in it, and it does, from a business perspective, innovation is just an act of will. *Let's build something better. Let's build something cooler. Let's build something bigger and badder and faster.* A better spear, a better assembly line, a better smartphone, a better company... you name it. If you care to improve it, you're a third of the way into the innovation process already.

You don't have to look far to see innovation in process every day. Look at athletics, for instance. We aren't talking about professional sports here, where huge R&D budgets go into making swimmers faster in the water, cyclists faster on their bikes and contact sport athletes safer from injury. We're talking about the sports and athletic endeavors many of us participate in, and the small innovations every day people come up with on a daily basis to improve performance and outcomes. Think, for example, of avid surfers who modify their boards or experiment with waxes. Think of snowboarders, skaters and BMXers who experiment with tricks and acrobatics. Think of all of the Crossfit-inspired gyms where athletes experiment with new skills, techniques and diet plans. All of that is innovation too. In most cases, the improvements that result from this constant experimentation doesn't turn into a product, service or technical innovation, but, in some cases, they do. New types of waxes enter the market regularly. Every season marks the introduction of new performance fabrics, new training techniques, new accessories, and new nutritional supplements. Innovation happens every single day. And, if you are passionate about your business, innovation should happen there every day as well.

FLIPPING THE SCRIPT ON "FAILURE"

Legend has it that Thomas Edison designed thousands of light bulb prototypes before he created one that could work as a mass-produced product. I imagine if he had taken the time to fail slowly instead of failing as fast as he could to get to where he was going.

Failure is not usually well regarded in the business world. Failure is thought of as a negative, the opposite of success, something to be punished for, admonished about, even fired over. As a result, a culture of fear has formed around the notion of failure, or, more specifically, the act of failing. Across tens of thousands of businesses every year, executives and their subordinates hide or minimize their failures, big and small, for fear of being sanctioned. From a young age, we are programmed to perceive failure as a negative and to avoid it at all cost.

Well, it's stupid. Time and time again, what we have learned from innovators is that failure drives breakthroughs. It doesn't matter if you're Edison obsessing over light bulbs, Michael Jordan perfecting his free throw or the team that will eventually discover a cure for cancer, failure is what gets us to success. Without it, we don't learn what works and what doesn't.

The trick to making failure work is threefold:

1. *You must fail with purpose. Failure is about experimentation and discipline. It isn't supposed to be a crapshoot. It's a scientific method of trial, error and discovery. You need a system for it to work for you.*

2. *You have to give yourself and your employees permission to fail. That means creating rules for failure, lanes for everyone to fail in the right context and the right incentives too. Getting this right requires a change in culture and some consistency across the organization, so innovators who were free to take chances in one department don't get fired when they bring that methodology to another department for whom failure is still a negative.*

3. *It's imperative to build efficiency and speed into the model. You can't just fail with purpose. You have to do it fast. Getting to success is a numbers game, just like cold-call sales. How many doors can you knock on in a day? How fast can you weed out the bad prospects to get to the good ones? Innovation through rapid failure uses the same mechanism. How fast you get through those first thousand bad light bulb designs determines how fast you get to the one that will change the world.*

Adapting to disruption and leveraging change to improve your market position both require this mindset. Learning how to fail fast in the pursuit of success is a critical operational skill and the correct operational approach. It enables innovation by giving organizations the freedom to think beyond how things have always been done and the confidence to disrupt themselves to improve and effectuate breakthroughs.

When Alan Mulally took over a flailing Ford Motor Company just more than 10 years ago, he discovered that executives were hesitant to share their failures honestly. Realizing how this mindset ultimately impacted Ford's ability to innovate and adapt to change, he made a stand to publicly celebrate bold, calculated failures to help build a new culture of learning and experimentation. This helped Ford get unstuck, and that simple decision helped the stalled Detroit giant to restart its innovation engine.

Starbucks gets raked over coals by the business press on a regular basis over its failed experiments—from putting music stores in its coffee shops to testing wine and beer bar concepts—but what we see in Starbucks' failures are bold exercises in market tests and mechanisms of opportunity discovery. They illustrate some of the company's most valuable traits: curiosity, the courage to try, and the discipline to pull the plug and try the next thing when something doesn't work out. These failures shouldn't be ridiculed or frowned at. They should be celebrated for what they really are.

For every one of Starbucks' failed experiments is one that paid off. Think back to Starbucks' early and inspired adoption of social media, for instance. It was fast and effective. Starbucks beat everyone and reaped enormous benefits early while most companies were still trying to explain Twitter to their executives. Starbucks' experimentation with phone apps is another example. Starbucks Mobile Order & Pay has been a major growth driver for the company, and an essential component of its loyalty-building strategy, especially among digital natives and millennials who enjoy using the app to order and pay. Starbucks' use of data to pinpoint ideal store locations and increasingly create customized experiences for its customers is also a way the coffee brand continues to remain competitive when other entrants in the category could threaten its dominance. Even Starbucks' seasonal drinks and themed cup colors started out as experimentation before they became tradition. Companies that give themselves permission to fail, and develop fail-fast experimentation models, tend to be more entrepreneurial, enjoy more breakthroughs than companies that don't, and adapt to changes in their business model with more agility and speed. It's that simple.

SECRET LABORATORIES VS OPEN ECOSYSTEMS OF INNOVATION: FINDING THE IDEAL BALANCE BETWEEN COMPETING MODELS OF INNOVATION

There are essentially two general models of innovation: the secret lab model and the open collaboration model. The secret lab model is built around traditional R&D: Hire scientists, engineers and designers, give them tools, funding and direction, and let them come up with the next round of innovation. Companies with cyclical product iterations tend to favor this model. Computer and phone companies, for instance, are expected to release new versions of last year's products every year or so. Automobile makers also. This year's model is different from last year's model, and, next year, they will introduce a new model. That requires dedicated teams of engineers, designers, product managers, quality control engineers, attorneys, and so on. Generally, the work these teams do is secret until the time comes to reveal what they have been working on. One could say that companies like Facebook and Amazon, and most software companies, really, operate the same way. New features, capabilities and services are quietly built inside the wire and unveiled when ready.

Open innovation is different. It tends to be far more collaborative and incremental. No one in that model is working on a super secret new design for anything. Open innovation fixes problems and improves inefficiencies. When Starbucks first started investing in Twitter in the early days of the platform, what Starbucks was practicing was an open form of innovation. Starbucks didn't build anything in a secret lab. The company simply saw an opportunity to leverage the 140-character, mobile-friendly, real-time communication social platform to engage with customers and potential customers. Inside of a year, Starbucks had one of the largest Twitter followings of any corporation or brand anywhere in the world, and it used that media platform to build loyalty, brand value, drive business, and address customer service issues transparently and in real time. As common as this use of Twitter may seem today, back then, Starbucks was a social media pioneer. No lab or R&D needed.

Open innovation sometimes also creates and defines industry standards (like safety standards, for instance, or best practices). This process can also live inside an organization. We've watched countless companies organically transition from email to collaboration apps, for example. Not because the CEO or COO sent out an email to the entire company and announced that Slack, Cisco Spark or some other mobile-friendly collaboration product would now be the *de facto* collaboration tool, but because project teams started experimenting with new tools and settled on something that worked better. As they shared their positive experiences and results with peers, the adoption of these tools began to spread. Over time, the process became formalized in one way or another, with IT getting involved, protocols set up, and so on. The point here is that this too is an example of open innovation.

Open innovation often also relies on the existence of IP (intellectual property) ecosystems where organizations can go to license technologies developed for their market by specialized technology companies, then use these technologies to build new products and services (or simply participate in the next technical evolution of their industry). Companies like Qualcomm, Intel, Nvidia, and ARM, which tend to favor secret laboratory innovation internally help fuel open innovation across dozens if not hundreds of industries by making their IP and products available to business customers. That's why you'll find Intel chips in hundreds of technology products like computers and smart watches, and Qualcomm hardware, software and IP in everything from smartphones and autonomous drones to smart TVs and smart city infrastructure.

Most companies, especially companies that operate in STEM (To Reiterate - Science, Technology, Engineering and Maths) industries, tend to do a little bit of both. But, even if you are a small, local company, the open innovation model is a treasure trove of opportunity for business leaders open to making full use of it.

Take healthcare, for instance. Healthcare and the IoT have, for some years now, found themselves on a collision course of possibly epic proportions. Consider the impact of embedded sensors, connectivity, edge computing, and the Cloud on a $4 trillion industry in dire need of new ideas and new solutions, especially in the United States, where access to health insurance and affordable healthcare is still precarious for many of people. Enter Qualcomm, one of the world's most prolific engines of innovation.

Most people have heard of Qualcomm, even if they don't know precisely what Qualcomm does. It is a big tech and telecommunications company that develops industry standards and licenses IP to pretty much every company that touches wireless communications. Its massive patent portfolio gets bigger every day. An easier way to look at it is to just ignore the telecom piece and think of Qualcomm as one of the world's most valuable and equal-opportunity R&D labs.

It wasn't always so. Like IBM and many other tech giants, Qualcomm used to be into hardware, infrastructure, software, IP, and so on. Qualcomm did it all, and it was too much. So little by little, Qualcomm shed unwanted weight and remade itself into an enabler of innovation—a platform company that thousands of other tech companies, as big as Apple and as small as the greenest startup, could come to for help about pretty much anything, from wireless connectivity and machine learning to sensor technology and thousands of other things besides. Qualcomm is also a true silicon/semiconductor company, and its chipsets and SOCs (System On Chip) are second to none. The company, started in 1985, has grown to $23 billion in annual revenue, and, as this book goes to print, somehow manages to ship roughly one million chips to the IoT industry every single day.

So what does Qualcomm have to do with healthcare? Well, given where healthcare is going, and the impact that the IoT is sure to have on that industry, a heck of a lot. But being the world's purveyor of useful IP and handy technology isn't enough. To lead in this new market, you need focus. You need purpose. You need vision. If you're Qualcomm, a company that has made a name for itself in the smartphone and telecommunications industries, how in the world do you transform healthcare? Or more to the point, if you want to translate this problem into one that is more relevant to your own company's current challenges, how do you take your decades of expertise in one industry and become a major player in another? It's hard. It's almost impossible, really, and few companies ever manage to pull it off.

But Amazon, Apple, IBM, and Tesla did… and, if you have been paying attention, you will notice that these companies come up a lot in these seven chapters. That's because futureproof companies tend to be able to leverage new technologies and innovation to jump into new categories and markets, and either take them over completely or be successful there. Qualcomm's approach here can teach us a few things about how to do it right.

1. Qualcomm create a business devoted to this healthcare tech movement. It's called Qualcomm Life. What this brings to the equation is specificity of purpose, focus and dedicated resources. Its mandate is clear—lead the way in the digitization of healthcare.

2. *Instead of just moving executives from various existing divisions to run this new group, Qualcomm hired some of the world's most experienced and talented healthcare professionals to work alongside its own researchers, IP specialists, and business leaders to shape the group's capabilities and steer it in the right direction.*

3. *Qualcomm started making its patent portfolio available to the biotech and pharma industries. Not that it wasn't before, but without focus and attention, things don't happen on their own. Touchpoints became conversations. Conversations became focused discussions. Focused discussions became strategies and pilot programs. Strategies and pilot programs grew into partnerships. Qualcomm Life is already partnering with healthcare leaders like Novartis, Philips, United Healthcare, and Walgreens to develop some of tomorrow's IoT and tech-powered healthcare solutions.*

As a footnote, there are roughly 15 billion mobile devices in the world. By 2022, there will be close to 50 billion connected devices in the world. Those won't all be phones, thermostats and smart speakers. They'll also be healthcare devices. Aside from smart home and general use consumer IoT devices that can be incorporated into a broad healthcare ecosystem (like IP cameras, tablets, home sensors, and phones), Qualcomm identified three specific categories of connected consumer-centric medical devices it wants to help companies develop and bring to market:

1. *Diagnostic devices*

2. *Therapeutic devices*

3. *Biometric devices*

These devices represent everything that can help quickly and reliably diagnose, treat and monitor health challenges, including connected inhalers, pill dispensers, heart rate monitors, blood pressure monitors, thermometers, pregnancy test devices, and tubes of ointment.

Why does anyone need a connected inhaler and a connected blood pressure monitor? Because of the improved opportunities for better care via telehealth and telemedicine, or as we prefer to refer to it: connected care.

Question 1: *Why waste time and go through the stress of a doctor's visit if you can monitor your own health from home, and have your medical data points upload directly to a healthcare solution powered by a specialized AI that will notify your healthcare provider of your status and make preliminary recommendations?*

Question 2: *How much time and cost can patients cut out of the healthcare equation if even 30 percent of their routine healthcare monitoring can be done reliably from home?*

Question 3: *How many more patients can a single doctor manage with a smart, partially automated ecosystem of patient management, data collection and deep analysis?*

Question 4: *More importantly, how much improvement in healthcare outcomes can we drive by making healthcare monitoring, management and diagnoses as easy as getting a patient to use an app on their phone or speak a command to a handheld device?*

I imagine being able to monitor whether patients are following their treatments.? Are they taking their pills? If so, are they taking them on time? Are they using the right amount of ointment? Are they exercising the way they ought to? Are they getting enough rest? Are they hydrating properly? Is their blood pressure elevated? Is their heart rate irregular? Sensors in everything can help healthcare providers monitor the effectiveness of a treatment, keep patients honest, make adjustments when needed, and intervene in case of an emergency. Biotech and Pharma companies, on their end, can develop new products and new delivery vehicles, track usage and the effectiveness of their products, and collect valuable data they can use to also drive positive outcomes.

Let's flip the script now and look at this from the perspective of pharma and biotechs. We aren't just talking about "Big Pharma" and "Big Biotech." We're also talking about startups, healthcare device manufacturers, and the broad ecosystem of businesses that stands to capitalize from the integration of the IoT in healthcare. You make a medical device like an inhaler or a birth control strip. You realize the potential that the IoT has for that category of product. You want to explore those possibilities, but you know nothing about the IoT, sensors, telemedicine, or healthcare apps. Who do you turn to?

Simple: You turn to companies that specialize in helping businesses like yours turn analog healthcare devices into digital ones. Companies like Qualcomm Life.

This means that you will have to create your own digital product group to manage that relationship and build that new piece of your business. Bear in mind that this group may, inside of five years, become the bulk of your business, and that if it is successful, you may see fast growth. This means that, aside from bringing new competencies and capabilities into your business to properly drive your new technology-driven model, you also will have to digitally transform your business to cope with the scale of your new endeavor and its change in operational velocity.

Our last observation is that, in a nascent and highly disrupted ecosystem like healthcare, once the IoT really starts shaking its foundations, organizations are going to have to learn how to collaborate (internally and externally) better than they ever have. Companies that figure out how to do this the fastest will enjoy a significant advantage over organizations that struggle with collaboration. Our advice is to start working on this now. Qualcomm, in its effort to operate as a universal technology enabler, built a partnership-friendly business model, but don't expect all partnerships in a volatile ecosystem to be easy and smooth right from the start. Plan for challenges.

Speaking of opportunities in healthcare and new paradigms of collaboration, let's also look at how HPE and GE Healthcare have found ways of leveraging digital transformation (and each other's core competencies) to create opportunities for themselves in tomorrow's connected healthcare industry.

First things first, here are some useful data points. We've already talked numbers a little bit, but here are a few more. GE Healthcare is an $18 billion per year company with 52 thousand employees in more than 100 countries. It has a big footprint, healthy market penetration, and isn't a bad platform if you have the right kinds of ideas to inject into a market hungry for innovation.

Now let's look at what HPE and GE are thinking about in terms of opportunity. Roughly 10 percent of the world's GDP is spent on healthcare each year. The world's 60-and-over population will double between now and 2050. There are more than 16,000 hospitals worldwide. Make a note of those numbers because they will help put this partnership in perspective.

Now let's talk about what GE Healthcare does. The GE subsidiary is a pharmaceutical and medical equipment company. It provides, among other things, imaging and information technologies, medical diagnostics, patient monitoring systems, and bio/pharma manufacturing technologies. If this reminds you of Qualcomm Life's three areas of focus (diagnostic, therapeutic and biometric), congratulations, you are paying attention.

Translation: GE Healthcare, as a global leader in medical imaging solutions, sees the technological transformation of healthcare as an opportunity to create some efficiencies in the way that hospitals and healthcare providers, store, manage, and share their digital records. It seems like a small, niche thing, but hospitals need systems that are secure, easy to use, talk seamlessly to each other, optimize workflows, and so on. The problem is that medical professionals are not IT professionals, and hospitals need to be able to focus on delivering care, not solving IT problems. If GE Healthcare can help hospitals streamline at least this aspect of their technology stack with a standardized, reliable and user-friendly technology solution for the management of PACs (Picture Archiving and Communications systems), that's a big opportunity for them, and a huge positive for hospitals and their patients.

The challenge is that while GE Healthcare is good at delivering imaging technology solutions, it isn't an IT infrastructure company.

There are bits and pieces of the overall solution it has to either out-source or provide through a technology partner.

HPE is the solution. If HPE supplies the IT hardware (space-efficient servers needed to run GE Healthcare's onsite PACs) to hospitals, that's one problem solved. Two, if HPE also provides IT expertise to hospitals through its HPE Pointnext services, which can be expanded to meet the hospital's own digital transformation needs, GE Healthcare can just focus on doing what GE Healthcare does best.

Think about it. What did GE Healthcare and HPE do here? They identified, in the disruption of an industry, an opportunity that made sense. They then partnered to create a joint solution that would solve a problem for more than 16,000 hospitals worldwide. They innovated. They adapted. They leveraged technology to build something new, valuable and profitable. The pitch to hospitals? Up to 40 percent in efficiency improvements. A 30 percent reduction in PAC configuration costs, and up to 20 minutes saved per procedure. (To understand the cumulative value of that last number, multiply it by 100,000 exams per year, if not double that.)

The lesson here is twofold:

1. *Futureproofing is, at its core, about looking for emerging threats and opportunities, and being able to adapt to meet those challenges hard and fast.*

2. *If you can't build a complete technology solution in-house, don't shelf the idea and don't put it off. Find a technology partner and build it with them*

GIANT LEAPS, REVOLUTIONS AND INCREMENTALISM

When talking about innovation, it is also important to consider how innovation happens over time. Generally, innovation comes in three distinct modes: Cyclical, incremental and disruptive revolutions.

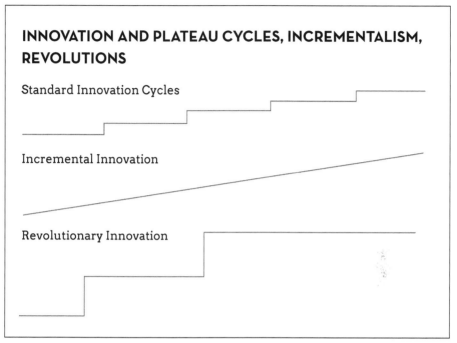

INNOVATION AND PLATEAU CYCLES, INCREMENTALISM, REVOLUTIONS

Standard Innovation Cycles

Incremental Innovation

Revolutionary Innovation

Innovation and plateau cycles (steps), incrementalism (diagonal), revolutions (vertical adjustments)

Cyclical innovation refers to the type of innovation cycles we just discussed: Computer, smartphone, automotive, and software companies releasing new and improved versions of their most popular products every year. New features, improved performance, new design characteristics, etc. Some of these cycles refresh quarterly, others are set to a 12-month cycle, and others (especially in industrial environments) can be years in the making. They are generally predictable though, which means they are usually minimally disruptive.

Incremental innovation is not cyclical. It is continuous. It tends to be the result of tinkering and internal process improvement. Examples of incremental innovation can be found in retail, industrial environments, financial organizations, and pretty much anywhere the fine tuning of a solution to a problem occurs continuously. Adjusting audience targeting for a category of content, for instance, is incremental innovation. Adjusting data inputs to optimize an analytics AI's predictive models is incremental innovation. The continuous application of lessons learned in the deployment of AR and VR tools in a design-focused engineering firm is incremental innovation. The steady growth of mobile payment solutions is also an example of incremental innovation.

Revolutionary innovation doesn't come in cycles. It tends to come irregularly and unpredictably, and is often the result of Eureka moments and breakthroughs that either may not have been easy to predict, or whose timing was unexpected or uncertain. Revolutionary innovation is the most disruptive type of innovation not only because it tends to strike without warning, but because it tends to also change the game, so to speak, for the industries it is relevant to. Ford's assembly line system, the one that shortened the automobile manufacturing process from 12 hours to under three hours was a revolutionary innovation. The personal computer was a revolutionary innovation. Television and the internet were revolutionary innovations. Anything that becomes a milestone separating "life before this invention" and "life after this invention" is revolutionary, from the introduction of the polio vaccine to the launch of Uber.

We mention these three categories of innovation because, to create cultures of innovation, we have to understand innovation, and to understand innovation, we have to understand its structure, mechanism and many forms. When we look at how innovation fits into the futureproofing of an organization, the mechanisms by which innovation happens are anchored in that organization's operational proclivities. Some organizations naturally operate in an incremental innovation mode. Other organizations naturally follow industry standards of cyclical innovation. More still (particularly tech startups and biotech companies) tend to pursue revolutionary innovation in the hopes of disrupting incumbent markets and creating entirely new categories of products, services and experiences.

No model is better than the other, and all three models can exist simultaneously in the same organization, so there is no reason for us to make a judgment call as to which type of innovation or which proportion of all three is best. Every company is unique. The one observation we will make, however, is this: The more risk-averse and "safe" a company is, the more likely it is to favor incremental innovation. The more opportunity-focused and driven a company is, the more likely it is to favor revolutionary innovation. In an age of constant technology disruption, companies have a choice to either disrupt or be disrupted. Companies that disrupt industries enjoy the initiative, and the initiative is always a tactical advantage. Disruptive companies are playing offense. Everyone else is playing defense. If you look at category leaders today, you will find that the market leadership they enjoy is always based on their having been the disruptors. For example:

- Apple disrupted the personal computer, the music player and the mobile phone industries.

- Amazon disrupted the bookseller, retail and smart speaker industries.

- Uber and Lyft disrupted the taxi industry.

- Airbnb disrupted the hotel industry.

- Websites like Orbitz, Expedia and Kayak disrupted the travel booking industry.

- Websites like Hotels.com and Trivago disrupted the hotel booking industry.

- Netflix disrupted the video rental industry.

- Facebook and Google disrupted the advertising and news industries.

Think about the companies that are hard at work to disrupt the healthcare, energy, utilities, grocery shopping, engineering services, legal services, accounting, strategic consulting, security, and entertainment industries. Is their internal focus on incremental innovation or on pursuing revolutionary innovation? What types of innovation cultures are they fostering? This is not an abstract or existential question. It's a practical one. And that question circles back to the most important question of all: What kind of company do you want to build? A category leader or an also-in company? A company that drives change or a company that is forced to weather it? A company that futureproofs itself by defining its *own* future on its own terms, or a company that prefers to react and adapt to external disruption? Again, we aren't making judgments. There is no right or wrong answer. As a business leader, you just need to know what the answer is, then create an innovation culture inside your organization that will help you deliver on that objective. It won't happen on its own. Someone has to build and nurture it.

NEW TECHNOLOGIES AND THE CHANGING PACE OF INNOVATION CYCLES

One of the most exciting opportunities we see emerging in the machine learning and cognitive computing space is the potential to help organizations minimize risk. Think about how people usually make decisions. On a good day, every decision is little more than an educated guess, right? Even when you have outstanding data and a solid understanding of your space, you always have to contend with a pretty big bucket of variables. Things could go wrong. Your pricing structure could be off. Your distribution strategy could be flawed. You might have overestimated the market's interest in your product or service. A competitor who was flying under your radar could come out of nowhere and suddenly displace a piece of business that you thought was secure. Every business bet is exactly that, a bet. It's a calculated risk. And, if you have worked around decision makers long enough, you know that they can have wildly different approaches to risk management.

Risk is binary. It triggers a fight or flight response in us all. For some, it's motivation to hit the gas. For others, it's a signal to hit the brakes. Decision makers, whether they're CEOs, team leaders or project managers, are no different. Some decision makers, motivated by the allure of their internal risk vs reward calculus, tend to be risk takers. Others decision makers, more focused on a fear of failure, tend to be far more cautious, often to the point of being risk averse. How machine learning, cognitive computing and AI impact the decision making process of these groups of decision makers is what we find particularly interesting.

When we talk about technology's impact on the pace of innovation, we are talking about velocity. Before we address the pace of innovation itself (research, development, design, testing, and so on), we have to focus on how technology can help increase decision-making velocity.

For starters, organizations that make good decisions fast tend to have an advantage over organizations that struggle with their decision-making process. We see this with companies that are quick to invest in new technologies and business models versus companies that take their time, play it safe, and, as a result, miss critical windows of opportunity to get into new spaces early.

One of the most underappreciated gifts of digital transformation is the ability it grants companies to virtualize not only design and engineering, but also trial and error.

One aspect of digital transformation that doesn't get mentioned enough is the extent to which access to technology expertise is now available to all. There's a reason tiny startups in Silicon Valley are able to turn themselves into billion dollar companies in short time spans. If you pay attention to some of the examples and case studies we inject into these chapters, you will notice that we reference innovation enablers more than once. Innovation enablers are companies that essentially act as R&D labs for entire industries, and provide companies that aren't necessarily the best at IT or technology research with the bits and pieces of the technology puzzle that will turn their big ideas into practical realities.

Among these companies are familiar names like Qualcomm, HPE, SAP, Intel, GE, and Dassault Systèmes. Since we are touching on the subject of virtualization, we want to give Dassault Systèmes a quick nod because, like many major technology enablers, they tend to take a back seat to the accomplishments of the clients whose disruptive ideas they turn into market wins. Dassault Systemes is essentially a 3D experience company. If you're an engineer or a designer, chances are you already use some of their products, like Solidworks, Catia, Simulia, and Geovia. It doesn't matter if you're designing a bolt for a machine press, running virtual crash tests on your new family car concept or working with city planners to figure out how to turn your downtown district into a case study in IoT integration best practices, Dassault's solutions power pretty much every aspect of innovation and design once the time comes to put ideas to paper.

One of their most interesting partnerships already helped medical researchers model the human heart to accelerate the design, testing and proofing of pacemakers, surgeries, medicines, and other life-saving interventions. Their products allow car manufacturers to virtually test their vehicles before they commit to physical crash tests, saving them massive amounts of time and money. By combining their various solutions, designers and engineers are able to accelerate advanced material, aeronautics, industrial, architectural, product, and retail experience design... there are virtually no limits to what these tools allow companies of all sizes to do. The rapid prototyping process that was revolutionary a decade ago has become entirely virtual, cost-effective and a lot faster than it once was. And, with the advent of virtual and augmented reality technologies, Dassault Systemes' solutions are about to become a whole lot more user-friendly and accessible.

Companies looking for technical help as they move forward with their digital transformation initiatives have to learn to work closely with technology enablers. We cannot stress enough the importance of this one insight. Even Apple doesn't go at it alone. No company has ever futurproofed itself by working alone. Amazon, Starbucks, Apple, Facebook, Burberry, Disney, Nike... it doesn't matter what company you study. Every single one has, at one time or another, and today still, relied on outside help from a technology enabler. It doesn't matter if it's an IP powerhouse like Qualcomm, a design software leader like Dassault Systemes, you stand to benefit by working with a digital transformation infrastructure partner like HPE, a data-driven solutions provider like SAP, or a niche pioneer like Meta. Identify these companies, find ways of partnering with them and let them solve some of your technology challenges for you.

Trial and error doesn't have to be expensive anymore. It doesn't have to take time and resources to test in the real world. Retail spaces can be modeled in photorealistic virtual environments that stakeholders and focus groups can walk through and interact with. The same technologies can be used to model the effectiveness of product launches and visualize the social content amplification of a tweet or social video based on channels and ad spend. As we write this book, the virtualization of trial and error isn't exactly new, but it hasn't gone mainstream quite yet either. By 2025, it will be a lot more common practice to use virtualization and powerful cognitive computing solutions to test ideas, model campaigns, identify unexpected problems and threats, and make better decisions. The sooner you start getting familiar and comfortable with virtualization tools, the better. Remember our earlier advice about not rushing change? *Slow is smooth; smooth is fast.*

Integrating this kind of technology into a business model that is unfamiliar with it isn't easy. The basics take time to master. Building new processes and methodologies around this takes time too. Don't wait. The sooner you start, the sooner that learning curve will flatten.

CHAPTER 5:

LEADERSHIP & TRANSFORMATION

The True Function of Leadership Isn't What You Think

TO BOLDLY GO - A NEW MODEL OF LEADERSHIP

"A competent leader can get efficient service from poor troops, while on the contrary, an incapable leader can demoralize the best of troops." – John J. Pershing

Leadership isn't management. Leadership is leadership. In the abstract, that is why we have CEOs and COOs and why those roles, while complementary, are vastly different. We don't mean to minimize the role of the COO. Far from it. COOs run the ship. They make sure that stuff gets done, that schedules and objectives are met, that the axles are greased and the tanks filled. COOs are vital to the planning and management of pretty much every moving part, big and small. They manage supply chains, logistics, technology, and people. Good CEOs ensure that the ship runs smoothly and reaches its objectives and destinations on time. On a smaller scale, managers perform a COO-like function. They make sure that things get done. If something gets in the way, they fix it. If a problem comes up, they address it. Being a manager requires planning, discipline, attention to detail, operational fluency, and a certain degree of agility that allows them to put out a never-ending onslaught of fires while always driving toward their goals.

And yet, while a capacity for leadership certainly is a sought-after quality among managers, leadership as a function rather than a trait exists apart from pure management functions. Think of the difference between a ship's captain and his XO. What does the captain do? What is his function? His function is to set objectives, to point to a destination on a map and decide the best way of getting there. If the ship runs into trouble, his crew looks to him to come up with a winning strategy. The actual running of the ship is delegated to the XO, however, and to the highly specialized hierarchy that makes the crew more than a random assembly of warm bodies.

Leadership as a function is instinctively understood in all social constructs. Even in highly communal societies, where decisions are made as a group, elders tend to be looked upon as leaders, for their wisdom, if nothing else. War chiefs are chosen to lead tribes into battle. Captains are appointed to command ships and lead crews. Directors are hired to direct movies and chefs to run restaurants. From Presidents to CEOs, we expect *leadership*. We *need* leadership. Why? Because leaders set the objectives, leaders keep us focused on achieving them, and, by sheer force of will, leaders motivate us to keep things moving forward and achieve the impossible.

When we ask people to make a list of their top 10 favorite leaders, or the world's greatest examples of leadership, the list invariably includes names like Martin Luther King, Alexander the Great, Joan of Arc, Julius Caesar, Steve Jobs, Winston Churchill, Napoleon, Cleopatra, George Washington, Spartacus, George Patton, Richard Branson, Walt Disney, and Abraham Lincoln. Aside from their fame and historical significance, what strikes us is that, regardless of the names that come up, the five most common traits these leaders share are:

1. They were all visionaries.

2. They were all risk takers.

3. They were all rulebreakers.

4. They were all change agents.

5. They were all immensely successful as a result of those four traits.

There is a lesson here if you are paying attention. They aren't known or looked up to for their amazing ability to organize a schedule or make the trucks run on time. The universal celebration (or at least, the acknowledgment) of their leadership isn't predicated on their overall management skills, but rather on specific *leadership* traits that people naturally are drawn to, admire and aspire to emulate. They are traits that ultimately translate into the kind of legendary success that most of us only dream of being part of.

If you haven't already noticed it, this combination of traits tends also to be found in every culture's most celebrated heroes, an insight we will revisit later in this chapter. For now, what we want to convey is that by studying what traits and characteristics make popular leaders great, we can better understand the general expectations that people place on leaders, and, since this is a business book after all, specifically on CEOs.

TRANSFORMATIONAL LEADERSHIP VS STATUS-QUO LEADERSHIP: AVOIDING THE MANAGEMENT TRAP

"Strategic leaders must not get consumed by the operational and tactical side of their work. They have a duty to find time to shape the future." - Stephanie S. Mead

The setting was a tech conference, specifically, a panel on leadership in the age of digital transformation. A prematurely graying corporate executive type in an aggressively tailored suit and sporting a clever smile caught the attention of the moderator, and asked the question he had been eager to ask for the better part of 20 minutes. "Can a CEO who champions the status quo still be considered a leader?" The panelists took turns answering the question. *Yes. No. Sort of.* Beyond the platitudes and the clichés, the question, it seemed, was never really answered. Not to his satisfaction anyway. Let's fix that. The answer is no.

A CEO who champions the status quo is not a leader. He or she is a custodian, a guardian. If there is no forward momentum, no exploration, no adaptation to change, you may have management, but you don't have leadership. Let's return to our five leadership traits for a moment. When a CEO champions the status quo, where is the vision? Where is the risk-taking? Where is the rule breaking? Where is the change agency? Where is the immense success resulting from boldly leading the organization toward new shores?

Another way to ask this question is: Would Steve Jobs have been *Steve Jobs* had he championed the status quo? How about Jeff Bezos? Howard Schultz? Walt Disney? Elon Musk? Marc Benioff? Mark Zuckerberg? Would we have Apple, Tesla, Amazon, Facebook, Google, Netflix, Uber, Airbnb, or Qualcomm if these companies were led by champions of the status quo? Would we have self-driving cars smartphones, social media, cloud computing, edge computing, mixed reality, artificial intelligence, or smart homes if the CEOs of the companies developing these technologies had simply sat back and managed their companies instead of leading them toward new horizons?

So there is no status-quo leadership. There can't be. Companies are like ships, they have to sail. When companies stop sailing, when they sit at anchor too long, they begin to rot. It's as simple as that.

Caveat: In times of incremental change, when disruption is unlikely, and the next evolutionary cycle may be years away, handing over a company to a change-or risk-averse CEO isn't necessarily a bad thing. It can be healthy for a company to go into maintenance mode, especially after a long, hard burn. That's when a COO taking the place of a CEO can actually be advantageous. Power down for a few quarters. Work on efficiency and process optimization. Focus on getting the details right again. Breathe. But in times of disruptive, fast-paced, brutal change, it's a bad idea. Status-quo CEOs, custodian CEOs, change-averse CEOs, risk-averse CEOs, wait-and-see CEOs, or manager-CEOs aren't equipped to lead companies forward or help them keep up with change, let alone position them to become more competitive. They lack the temperament required to pull it off. This isn't a critique, mind you. It's merely an honest and pragmatic observation. They may be fantastic managers, first rate COOs, but they simply aren't wired to race into the storm to gain an advantage over their competitors. It takes a different kind of mentality and skillset to do that.

This means that true leaders are *always* transformational and change agents, so great CEOs are always in the process of reinventing their companies for whatever comes next. Tesla, Apple, IBM, and Amazon didn't start as the companies they are now. Tesla's Hyperloop came later. Mixed Reality and smartphones isn't what Apple built its brand on. Artificial Intelligence wasn't IBM's bread and butter 30 years ago. Amazon used to sell books, now it sends rockets into space. Leaders know that no organization can achieve what no one else has as long as it clings to old ideas, processes, methodologies, and skillsets. In order to break new ground, they must be pioneers. They must experiment. They must try and fail, then fail better and faster until they discover new ways to solve problems and smarter ways to succeed. Preserving the status quo is the antithesis of this mentality. It anchors companies in place. It weighs them down. It prevents them from moving forward. When an organization's survival depends on its ability to move forward as quickly and swiftly as possible, a CEO focused on preserving the status quo becomes a liability. It's that simple.

MUST THE CEO ALSO BE THE CHIEF TRANSFOR-MATION OFFICER?

"If you're not stubborn, you'll give up on experiments too soon. And if you're not flexible, you'll pound your head against the wall and you won't see a different solution to a problem you're trying to solve." – Jeff Bezos

Now that we have clearly demarcated leadership in times of disruption and change, the question that begs asking is "must the CEO also be the Chief Transformation Officer?"

The answer is yes.

The CEO sets the vision and the goals. The CEO articulates the plan and expectations to the staff. The degree to which the direction and purpose of said transformation and adaptation are clearly communicated, their importance appropriately stressed, their execution championed, and adequate resources assigned, all falls on the shoulders of the transformative CEO. "I want our company to be No. 1 in customer satisfaction" is a CEO objective. "I want our collaboration ecosystem to be 100 percent mobile friendly and app based by H2 of next year" is a CEO objective. "I want our retail spaces to be known for their unique use of mixed reality, AI and highly personalized shopping experiences" is a CEO objective.

The CEO sets the direction, goals and tone. Therefore, the CEO must take on the role, at least in spirit, of Chief Transformation Officer.

Here's a an example from GE. *To futureproof itself, GE realized that it had to do more than just upgrade its technology. It also had to adopt a digital first culture. What does that mean? Let's see if we can break it down into easily digestible parts.*

1. *During his tenure as CEO, Jeff Immelt expected his senior executives to spend roughly half a day with him every month to discuss and review every digital process and product under their care. This created a culture of mutual digital accountability at GE, and placed the organization's digital transformation responsibility squarely on the shoulders of its senior leadership. Using this method, there was no way that a senior decision maker at GE could be a technology laggard or luddite.*

   This model of sitting down with the boss to review all things digital ensures competence, focus and technology fluency. It's bold, and it's brilliant.

2. *Building on our previous point, GE's CEO essentially acted as the company's chief digital officer. Think about that, a CEO who actively drives digital transformation and holds his senior staff personally accountable for their part in it. We can't think of a better model than this.*

Independently of every other digital transformation investment, focus or activity made by GE in recent years, these two points deserve their own mention in this chapter because they so perfectly address the importance of leadership and ownership in all.

This isn't to say that the CEO should manage transformation and change across the organization, mind you. *Change management* is, as the term suggests, a management function. Its execution is best delegated to change management experts and junior leaders with operational transformation experience. The day-to-day planning and execution of the minutiae of transformation and adaptation—from employee training and process experimentation to technology acquisition and solutions integration—can't and shouldn't be the CEO's focus. The organization as a whole, in order to change, adapt and evolve, must learn to change, one skill at a time, one task at a time and one project at a time. Everyone in the organization must be responsible for planting, nurturing and cultivating the seeds of transformation.

An important point we should touch on is that adaptation typically happens at the individual level before it can happen at the organizational level. Ideally, the CEO, as the chief visionary, risk-taker, rule-breaker, change agent, and success engineer, is the first to begin to adapt, evolve and transform. If change were a virus, the CEO would be patient zero. Change, you see, is always born out of an idea, an exciting idea that could change the world. "What if we made computers fun and easy to use?" "What if we made electric cars that outperform even high-end luxury sports cars?" "What if we created magical experiences that made adults feel like kids again?" "What if we completely reinvented how people shop and pay for things?" "What if we could make going to space affordable and safe?" "What if we sailed west and proved, once and for all, that the Earth isn't flat?"

"What if" is an idea virus, the good kind, and it is the spark that sets alight every single transformative journey. "What if we stopped acting like a second-tier company?" "What if we started working smarter instead of longer?" "What if we didn't play it safe this one time?" "What if we aimed for the bleachers, just this once?" That's the stuff that makes CEOs like Jobs, Branson, Bezos, and Musk legends in the business world, and, in every single case, the idea virus infected them long before it infected anyone else who worked for them.

The thing about leadership is that it has to inspire, seduce and convert. For people to commit to following a path, especially one that comes with its own set of risks, professional or otherwise, they have to believe in an idea. They have to feel a swell of excitement for that idea. Something has to stir inside of them. They have to want to be part of it, part of the journey, the adventure, the experiment, and, hopefully, the success too when it finally comes. If they see that their CEO is 100 percent infected by this idea, 100 percent dedicated to its success, and they begin to see that it really could change the world for the better in some way, they will be far more likely to want to be a part of it too. Most people want to make a positive difference in the world. Most people want to know that their work matters. There is enormous power and potential in the universal desire to be helpful, relevant and valuable. A leader who empowers an organization to tap into that and turn it into focus, passion, zeal, and professional purpose can achieve anything. The ability to infect even the lowest ranking member of an organization with the same excitement and faith in an idea as the CEO, *that* is the essence of leadership.

HOW PERSONAL JOURNEYS IMPACT BUSINESS SUCCESS

"Good leaders organize and align people around what the team needs to do. Great leaders motivate and inspire people with why they're doing it. That's purpose. And that's the key to achieving something truly transformational." - Marillyn Hewson

It stands to reason that the roots of transformative leadership are firmly planted in personal journeys. Here is what we mean. On one hand, every transformation is, in and of itself, a journey, with a beginning, middle and end. (And, if not an end, at least a clear milestone that can close out a significant chapter of that journey.) On the other hand, every journey is a catalyst for adaptation and, therefore, transformation.

Here's an interesting little tidbit. Every successful CEO and every gifted leader is a terrific storyteller. Every single one, without fail. Here's why. Leaders like Musk, Branson, and Schultz all understand where they started, how far they've come and what it took to get there. They all have a deep appreciation for the journey they've been on and for the story of that journey. Sooner or later, they've all come to a point in their lives when they began to see how every action, every decision, every stroke of luck, every time they went left instead or right, or hit the gas instead of the brakes, or said yes instead of no, fits into the daisy chain of events that make up their personal story, and how that story weaves itself into the stories of the products, companies and successes they've had. The failures also have a place in those narratives. They're the learning moments. It's all there, it all matters and there's a tremendous amount of value to telling the bits and pieces of that story because everything that matters to them. Everything that has ever mattered and will ever matter is right there. There's a reason successful leaders write memoirs and why publishers fight over exclusive rights to publish their biographies. People want to know why they did what they did, how they did it, how they conquered adversity to beat the odds, came back from their failures, and eventually became the men and women they became. Those stories matter because they contain insights, secrets and lessons that anyone who hears or reads them can apply to their own lives. Those stories also matter because they connect us in predictable yet unexpected ways. They intersect with our own and reveal how much we have in common with our heroes, how much we share without really being aware of it.

Every successful CEO started out as a child with a quirk, challenge or talent. Every successful CEO had to abandon a childhood dream and found a new passion through a stroke of luck, a chance meeting or an unexpected connection. Every successful CEO failed spectacularly at least once, was humiliated and broken, thought their career was over, and came back to build something extraordinary. They battled enemies along the way and earned the loyalty of trusted allies. They pressed on when others wouldn't have and everyone told them they were mad. The stories are all different and unique, but, at their core, the elements are always the same. The structure is similar. The world's most accomplished and talented athletes, actors, scientists, politicians, and generals all have similar stories, similar journeys, similar tests of character and perseverance, and tests of overcoming failure and self-doubt.

Stories and personal journeys matter because we all have them too. We are what we overcome as much as what we achieve. We are the product of where we come from as much as of what we've built. None of what we do has meaning unless told and understood by way of a story. And, since every story is itself a journey, and every journey is a tale of transformation, personal journeys are at the heart of every business success. There is no escaping the power of stories and the unique journeys of a company transforming from what they were to what they aspire to be. We understand the value of things like achievements and sacrifice by learning the story of how they came to be. It's how, as a species, we have processed the world around us since the first fire burned in the first cave.

We need heroes and heroes need stories. If we are to be the heroes of our own stories, we need to be inspired, taught, and shown the way. Stories about visionary leaders give us permission to dream big. Stories about risk takers give us permission to be brave. Stories about rule breakers give us permission to color outside the lines and forge our own paths. Stories about change agents give us permission to try new things. Stories of success give us permission to hope and inspire us to become more than what we are. Success is, if nothing else, a journey of transformation. Unlike wealth and privilege, no one is born with success, or in it. It has to be fought for and earned. The decision to fight for it, to pursue it, to do whatever it takes to achieve it, doesn't happen without a catalyst of some kind.

How did Travis Kalanick and Garrett Camp get the idea for Uber? Legend has it that they were in Paris, attending *LeWeb*, wondering what the next big thing would be. This was December 2008. Camp was complaining about the taxi situation in San Francisco and wanted to create a sort of limo service you could summon by way of an iPhone app. A few months later, Camp was back in San Francisco, working on his idea. During the next few years, the concept evolved into the Uber we know today, but the original idea was just to get around the annoying problem of finding a cab at all hours and wanting to ride in cleaner, nicer and more comfortable cars.

Amazon's origin story is a little different. In 1994, Jeff Bezos was working on Wall Street. Web usage at the time was growing at more than 2,000 percent per year, and Bezos saw an opportunity to make a lot of money. Unlike Kalanick and Camp, Bezos wasn't trying to solve a nagging problem. He was looking for an in. His in was book sales; a low cost, high demand opportunity. It could have been anything. Electronics, apparel, shoes... but he chose books. It was a purely entrepreneurial business decision. Within a month of its launch, which he financed with savings, Amazon.com was averaging $20,000 per week in sales. Less than a year later, Bezos raised $8 million in funding. Two years later, in 1997, Amazon went public at $18 a share. It hasn't stopped growing and pushing its own limits since.

Every great company has an origin story, and every CEO and inventor does too. The investment banker who saw the internet as a potential goldmine, the tech entrepreneurs who set out to solve a nagging problem, a couple of engineers tinkering with prototypes in their garage, the inventor whose first 200 business ideas went nowhere but never quit, the kid with dyslexia who built a global superbrand... Personal journeys matter. They explain why. They inspire. It's unusual to find truly innovative, successful, courageous companies that don't have good stories to tell about their humble or otherwise unlikely beginnings.

SWORDS, STONES AND THE IMPORTANCE OF STORIES

"You have to look at leadership through the eyes of the followers and you have to live the message. What I have learned is that people become motivated when you guide them to the source of their own power and when you make heroes out of employees who personify what you want to see in the organization." - Anita Roddick

Stories give everything meaning. That's important because most people want their life to have meaning. Most people *need* their lives to have meaning. And so most people want their work to have meaning also. Few things in life are more soul sucking than working long hours at a boring, thankless job or for a company you don't love or believe in. Plotting this on a long enough timeline, no one wants to look back at a period of their lives, let alone an entire career, and feel that it was all meaningless.

This has nothing to do with how much money someone makes, or what the "seniority" of the job is. We aren't talking about janitors versus CEOs. We bumped into countless blue-collar workers who find purpose in their jobs, who love what they do, who find meaning in it, despite society oftentimes looking down on them for not being more "successful" or ambitious. Their upbeat attitudes and work ethic can be infectious though, and their personal stories are often inspiring. Conversely, we also have met countless well paid white collar workers, many of them senior executives, who hate their jobs and are generally bored with their lives, despite having risen to positions of responsibility and authority. Success hasn't made them happy. Money hasn't made them happy. What they do every day doesn't make them happy. Sit down with them long enough, and you'll start to notice a common thread in their stories—something missing. It's a shortage of meaning or a scarcity of purpose.

Meaning matters the same way purpose matters. Without it, you're just going through the motions. And, if you are just going through the motions, you aren't going to be able to drive any sort of meaningful transformation or help your organization become futureproof.

FORM FOLLOWS FUNCTION. PURPOSE INFORMS DIRECTION: REFRAMING THE PURPOSE AND FUNCTION OF LEADERSHIP

"I learned to always take on things I'd never done before. Growth and comfort do not coexist." - Ginni Rometty

This seems like as good a time as any to reframe our understanding of leadership, and establish some clear, sound and simple foundations. Let's break this down into eight digestible insights.

INSIGHT #1: THE PRIMARY PURPOSE OF GOOD LEADERSHIP IS TO MAKE AND DRIVE GOOD DECISIONS.

Our primary purpose isn't to "manage" people or organizations. While management and leadership can exist simultaneously, they are not interchangeable. *Leading* is about setting a destination and getting your organization from here to there. *Managing* is the process of making sure that the resources assigned can get the job done.

First and foremost, leadership must be about trust. An organization should be able to trust that the direction in which they are going, not to mention the actual destination, will pay off. The more leaders show they can make good decisions consistently, the more likely it is their organizations will trust in their leadership. Leaders who don't demonstrate the ability to make consistently good decisions will find themselves replaced by others who can.

The primary purpose of leadership, then, is to make good decisions.

INSIGHT #2: THE PRIMARY PURPOSE OF GOOD DECISIONS IS TO DRIVE POSITIVE OUTCOMES.

Good decisions about destinations and the paths we take to reach them ultimately drive outcomes. What happens when you reach that destination? Was it a good decision to embark on the journey in the first place? Decisions result in outcomes, and outcomes can be measured. Is the outcome a net positive or a net negative? Can the success or failure of the outcome be quantified? (When it comes to business, the answer should always be *yes*.)

INSIGHT #3: WE CANNOT TALK ABOUT LEADER-SHIP, GOOD OR BAD, WITHOUT FOCUSING ON BUSINESS OUTCOMES.

Good leadership is measurable. Leadership drives outcomes, and because those outcomes can be quantified, so can the leadership that drove them.

This point is vital to understand as we begin to shift our attention to data-driven leadership. Results, not merely good intentions, are the measure of effective leadership. A friendly boss isn't necessarily a good leader. A charismatic, well-spoken, inspirational executive is not necessarily a good leader, either. Even vision and intelligence don't necessarily make a CEO a good leader. These traits certainly are a plus, but, unless an individual in a leadership role can deliver quantifiable results that are aligned with business objectives, that individual is not an effective leader.

The measure of an effective leader, then, is his or her ability to drive relevant, meaningful and quantifiable business outcomes. Furthermore, driving positive business outcomes is a process. As with all processes, driving consistency should be a primary goal.

INSIGHT #4: CONSISTENCY IS NOT AN AFTER-THOUGHT OR A FOOTNOTE. IT IS A MEASURE OF EFFECTIVE LEADERSHIP.

If being right 50 percent of the time is better than being right 25 percent of the time, then being right 100 percent of the time is the ultimate goal of every decision maker. The question then becomes: How does a decision maker go from being right half the time to being right all the time? What best practices and tools can be applied toward this goal?

Consistency drives cycles. These cycles can either be *vicious* or *righteous*. Vicious cycles drive a series of *negative* outcomes. Righteous cycles drive a series of *positive* outcomes.

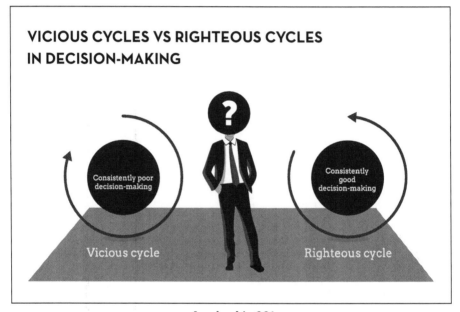

Leadership 001

The effectiveness of an organization's leadership is gauged by its business outcome cycles. Vicious cycles obviously point to a consistent failure rate, which indicates problems with the organization's decision-making model. Righteous cycles indicate the opposite: effective leadership driving positive outcomes.

With a deeper dig into righteous cycles, an organization can quantify outcomes to gauge whether the leadership has improved its decision-making ability over time, which can be an important operational insight.

IDENTIFYING VICIOUS CYCLES AND RIGHTEOUS CYCLES WITH DATA

Leadership 002

INSIGHT #5: MAKING BETTER DECISIONS THAT DRIVE CONSISTENTLY POSITIVE BUSINESS OUT-COMES IS THE BIGGEST CHALLENGE FACING BUSINESS LEADERS TODAY.

Whether the focus of the day is to accelerate digital transformation, improve customer retention, boost employee morale, or invest in the right product strategy, the primary worry of every decision maker is the same: *What if I'm wrong?*

This question has always haunted leaders. There is no such thing as a crystal ball in business. For centuries, making decisions has relied mostly on hunches, educated guesses, probability models, and a lot of crossed fingers and hoping for the best. Win some, lose some, repeat. The not knowing if they made the right decision or the right investment is what continues to keep executives, entrepreneurs and business owners up at night.

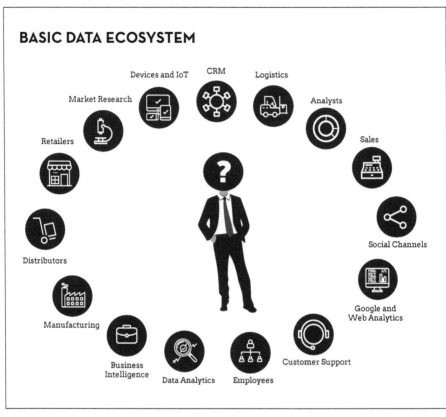

Leadership 003

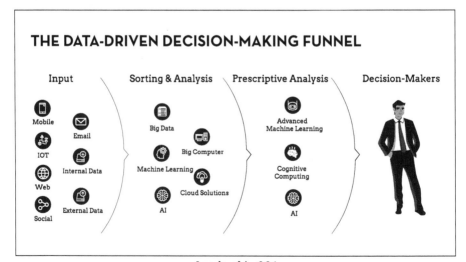

Leadership 004

The challenge for leaders and decision makers then is to improve their ability to consistently make better decisions. Here are some ways they can do it:

- Surround themselves with top-notch advisors and analysts,

- Invest in better business and market intelligence tools,

- Improve the quality of their data,

- Improve the quality and velocity of their data analysis,

- Invest in top-notch innovative talent that is aware of the market's ebbs and flows, and

- Adopt and implement successful methodologies and processes.

Put these options together and you get an ecosystem that can help decision makers improve the likelihood of positive outcomes.

INSIGHT #6: HAVING ACCESS TO BETTER DATA AND INFORMATION PROVIDES DECISION MAKERS WITH A SIGNIFICANT STRATEGIC ADVANTAGE.

We live and work in the information age, which means data is power. Decision makers need accurate data to know where to go next or how to respond to threats and crises. Given the preponderance of data available to decision makers now, as well as significant advances in data visualization, data analysis and predictive modeling tools, there is nothing standing in the way of creating data-driven leadership ecosystems.

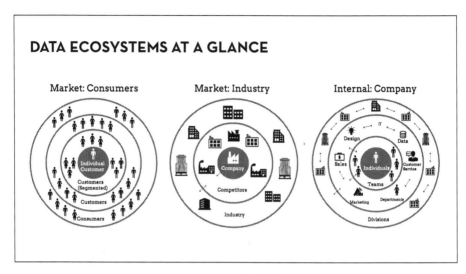

Leadership 005

Executives who embrace the value of data, understand the role data plays in making informed business decisions, and invest in data-driven ecosystems have a better chance of consistently positive business outcomes than executives who rely mostly on gut feelings, instincts and experiences. There is no organization anywhere on Earth that benefits from knowing *less* about its market and the world around it. In business, ignorance is *not* bliss.

INSIGHT #7: SHIFTING FROM A DECISION-MAKING MODEL BASED ON INSTINCT TO A DECISION-MAKING MODEL DRIVEN BY DATA IS NO LONGER HINDERED BY COST OR TECHNICAL LIMITATIONS.

One of the most significant barriers of technology adoption for senior executives traditionally has been the perception that technology is complicated. To a certain extent, this is true, but, thanks to an increase in the consumerization of IT, this is no longer the case, or at least not nearly as much as it once was. Data analysis, data visualization and predictive modeling tools are now much more accessible and user friendly than they were even a year ago, and they don't require deep or complex technical knowledge to use. This is especially true of solutions designed specifically for executives and senior leadership roles.

Moreover, most of these tools now live in the cloud and are offered as a SaaS model, effectively lowering, if not eliminating, traditional financial barriers of entry. It doesn't matter if you are a Fortune 500 enterprise or an SMB with a narrow local footprint, data-driven decision-making tools are available for every type of organization, every line of business (LoB), every market and vertical, and every budget.

Don't worry, we will take a closer look at the operational relationship between digital technologies and data-driven leadership in Chapter 6. For now, though, let's finish our leadership discussion.

The two biggest obstacles when it comes to adopting a data-driven decision-making model today are *mindset* and *culture*. As both tend to be rooted in the upper tiers of organizations that struggle with this technological shift, it falls on leaders and decision makers to overcome their own discomfort and preconceptions about technology to adopt and build effective, competitive and successful decision-making ecosystems for their organizations.

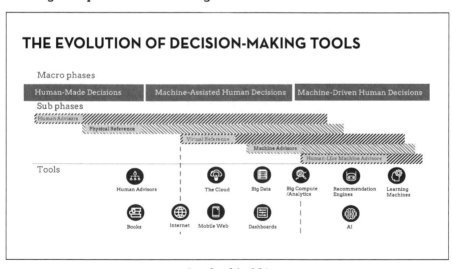

Leadership 006

The first step to addressing the issues of mindset and culture is to acknowledge that they exist.

The second step is to get to the root of the objections that drive any resistance to change. Identify the objections, address the objections, find adequate solutions to those objections, and finally agree on a plan to enact these solutions.

The third and final step is to remove any and all obstacles to the organization's journey of adaptation and improvement. This may require investments in education and skill development, product training, new processes and staff roles, technology, and a transformation roadmap that focuses specifically on this adaptive phase.

INSIGHT #8: OVERCOMING RESISTANCE TO CHANGE IS A KEY FUNCTION OF LEADERSHIP.

For better or for worse, responsibility is a staple of leadership. One bad bet or poor decision can cost people their jobs, make investors lose millions of dollars or set a company's mission back years. This is why change is hard. After all, change is always a risk as much as it is an opportunity. While opportunity gets leaders out of bed in the morning, it's risk that keeps them up at night.

Transitioning from gut feelings and instinct to soulless data and software is no different. It isn't just change, it is also an abdication of power. Leaders who believe in their own ability to make good decisions are suddenly asked to trust in machine and processes, which means they need to surrender some of their own power. That isn't easy. It takes a good deal of courage, work and testing to get to a point where decision makers can truly trust new technologies and tools. This aspect of digital transformation and technological adaptation shouldn't be minimized. It is the source of major resistance from executives, and it is a valid objection to the risk that "gut-feeling" leaders take when they shift to decision making driven by data and technology.

Another source of resistance among executives manifests itself as denial. It's the "everything is fine" objection to change. A 2015 study by the Global Center for Digital Business Transformation [10] found that 45 percent of business leaders didn't feel that digital disruption is a board-level concern. Forty-three percent felt that their company's leadership

---

[10]Bradley, J., Loucks, J., Macaulay, J., Noronha, A., & Wade, M. (2015, June). *Digital Vortex: How Digital Disruption is Redefining Industries* (Rep.).

either didn't recognize digital disruption as a concern or wasn't reacting to it appropriately, while 32 percent felt that their company was taking a follower approach. Only 25 percent reported that their company was actively responding by disrupting their own business.

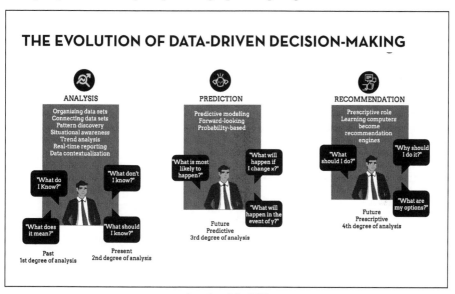

Leadership 007

Whenever resistance to change gets in the way of this process, always go back to your data. Are the company's outcomes currently in a vicious cycle or a righteous cycle? If it's a righteous cycle, are business outcomes improving or are they flat? How much room is there for improvement? What is the opportunity cost of not working toward better business outcomes?

Don't hesitate to validate your purpose for driving positive transformation in your organization as often as needed. The use of data to drive decision making is an effective proof of concept in and of itself.

In the end though, data won't convince people who don't want to be convinced. You have to be prepared for that. There will be people in every company who will dig in their heels and resist change. No matter how well you explain why things have to change, no matter how good your argument is, they will not go where you want them to. This is not necessarily a failure of leadership. Some people just aren't ready, and they are never going to be ready. As a transformational leader what matters more? Holding on to the past or building a better company for the future? It's a simple choice.

Here's a good example. In 2004, LEGO was on the brink of bankruptcy. The company had lost its focus. LEGO was making products, not creating experiences. It had let the connective tissue that linked it to its customers and fans wither away and die, and had squandered brand loyalty that had taken decades to build. LEGO didn't need a rebranding or a reimagining. It just needed a reboot. Jørgen Vig Knudstorp, then only 35, took over the company as CEO and gave it exactly what it needed. How did he do it?

- By refocusing the brand on its core business. If you can no longer do what you are known for well, you aren't ready to wander off into new markets and product categories. Before LEGO could start expanding again, it had to shed dead weight and prioritize.

- When video games started disrupting the toy industry, LEGO was among the first toymakers to start making video games. Those games had always enjoyed some measure of success, but, in 2005, LEGO released *LEGO Star Wars: The Video Game*, capitalizing on *Star Wars* fever and a risky but clever bit of licensing innovation. The success of the initial *LEGO Star Wars* mashup led to sequels, but also started a trend. LEGO also added *Indiana Jones*, *Batman*, *Pirates of the Caribbean*, *Harry Potter*, *The Lord of the Rings*, and Marvel to its roster of licensed properties. The idea was pure genius. Many other companies might have passed on it, preferring to not risk diluting the brand, but LEGO took a chance and it paid off.

- The backstory of how LEGO pushed through its years of lackluster success in the videogame industry is too long to go into here, but the main insights are:

- LEGO partnered with the right people – first with *TT Games*, then with *Warner Bros. Interactive Entertainment* when the media giant acquired TT games. If you can't develop the technical specialization you need in-house, find a partner.

- LEGO finally started thinking like a platform company. Licensing and crosslicensing are great ways to expand a brand's reach. If people love LEGO, and people love *Star Wars*, it stands to reason that LEGO + *Star Wars* = opportunity. LEGO tested the concept and the rest, as they say, is history.

- LEGO learned from its success with video games and took its entertainment and content play to new levels with feature-length movies (in partnership with Warner Animation Group), in addition to an expansion of its direct-to-video, TV specials and TV series portfolio.

- LEGO also saw how online commerce was changing retail, and started rebuilding its business ecosystem to focus on online and mobile retail rather than the brick-and-mortar distribution model the company, like most other retailers, had been based on since its launch.

- LEGO also endeavored to become a digital enterprise. To be competitive, the organization had to internally transform into a digital company.

- LEGO also focused on creating a flatter management structure that would be less hierarchical than it had traditionally been, making employees more empowered to act and adapt to stresses and opportunities quickly. One of the ways LEGO makes this work is by emphasizing simplicity and clarity of communications between its cadre of business leaders centered around organizational goals, targets, priorities, capabilities, and datasets.

- LEGO's culture is also once again 100 percent focused on serving, educating and entertaining children. This means that LEGO doesn't just manufacture products. LEGO designs experiences. This shift in focus, which infuses every facet of the company's culture with clear, shared purpose ensures that LEGO is always relevant to the market it serves (children), no matter what new technologies and disruptions leap out of the proverbial bushes in the future.

CHAPTER 6:

TECHNOLOGY

How New Technologies Are Transforming the World Around Us, and What To Do About It

Harnessing New Technologies to Improve Outcomes and Transform Businesses

Futureproof companies don't use technology like other companies. Their relationship to it is completely different.

To illustrate this, let's look at some of the ways that companies like Amazon, Uber, Facebook, and Airbnb are different when it comes to their use of technology.

1. *Digital is at the center of their business models. For them, it's digital first, not digital later. Digital isn't an add-on. It's core.*

2. *They use data differently. With digital first companies, every customer touchpoint is digital. And when every customer touchpoint is digital, every interaction with customers captures data: What they clicked on, what they swiped*

over, where they lingered, where they scrolled down, what they liked and didn't like, where they were last time they engaged with your company, where they usually are, how often, and so on. That amount of data requires a data-centric technology stack and a data-centric business culture. These two elements combined is what gives these companies the ability to market to consumers so much better than everyone else. When you can create accurate profiles and behavioral models of every single customer you have ever done business with, you have something most businesses don't.

3. They customize experiences and services for every customer. Note that Amazon's home page is a personalized dashboard, not a generic digital storefront. Are there common navigation and content elements that every visitor sees? Sure. But the recommendations, the welcome message and the search history layers are all unique to you, the visitor. Same with Facebook: That's your feed, your wall and your dashboard when you log in. When you open up your Uber app, the map shows where you are. The app is essentially your personal dashboard. That focus on deep customization is different from the way that other businesses, businesses that are still in the process of bolting digital on to their business model, approach digital design and integration.

Note that the biggest and most disruptive tech-driven companies—Google, Amazon, Facebook—also all use machine learning and AI to run their IT infrastructure, not just to process, manage and analyze content. This denotes a trend. Pay attention to it. Talk to your IT leadership team about it. If you have a CDO and/or a CIO on board, set up a meeting. This is not a detail. AI and machine learning helping your organization run its technology infrastructure, as opposed to not, is a gamechanger.

Lastly, they were all doing this before anyone else was.

WHAT TECHNOLOGIES SHOULD BE PART OF A TRANSFORMATIVE, FUTURE-PROOF, TECHNOLOGY-DRIVEN ECOSYSTEM?

The technologies every company currently should be focusing on can be broken down into the following categories:

- Mobility,

- Big Data/Compute/Analysis,

- Machine Learning/Cognitive Computing/AI,

- Cloud and Edge IoT,

- Augmented, Virtual and Mixed Reality,

- Industrial Automation,

- Blockchain, and

- Smart Collaboration Tools.

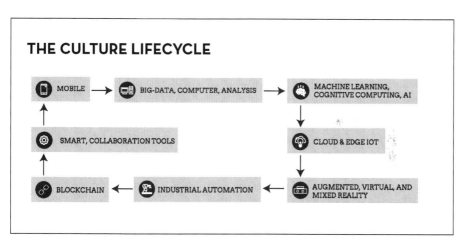

Leadership 008

CEOs, corporate boards and senior executives have to partner with CIOs and CTOs to put together a cohesive, results-driven technology adoption roadmap that meets the company's readiness plans for 2020 and 2025.

We have already touched on a number of these technologies in previous chapters and looked at how different companies that may not have always been the most digitally fluent still managed to leverage them to transform themselves into competitive, futureproof technology companies.

Part of this task, and one that we haven't focused nearly enough on yet, involves identifying technology solutions designed to improve decision making across the organization. These solutions exist to provide decision makers with access to pertinent data, as well as tools that can help them transform this data into actionable insights. No company can afford to fly blind, and no company this side of 2015 should have to. Data is the lifeblood of business now, so decision makers need dashboards they can use to make smart, fast and effective decisions.

Enter executive dashboards: Though new entrants in this space are common, Klipfolio, Domo, Sisense, Qlik, and Tableau are a good place to start for most SMBs, as they are easy to work with, and organize and deliver data in a way that decision makers can understand. The data they need is prefiltered and cleanly organized on one (or several) screens. Enterprise-level solutions providers like SAP, IBM, Salesforce, Dassault Systemes, Microsoft, HP Enterprise, and Oracle also provide robust BI dashboards for executives who prefer a more unified business software ecosystem. There is no right or wrong approach. Our perspective is that IT departments should test and review them all, and make routine recommendations to the departments and groups they work with whenever something new and exciting catches their eye.

On the front end, an executive dashboard's effectiveness is gauged by its ability to deliver data in a clear and coherent manner to a decision maker facing a deadline. To a secondary extent, it is gauged by its ability to allow said decision maker to dig deeper into a business-specific topic. On the back end, the effectiveness of such a dashboard relies on its ability to integrate with multiple sources of data, from Google Analytics, social media channels and sales systems to CRM, IoT and whatever other sources happen to be available. In either regard, not all dashboards are created equal.

If this all sounds complicated, it isn't. Well... it doesn't have to be. Executive dashboards are becoming increasingly customizable, allowing decision makers to select the types of data they want and what types of visualizations are best to qualify and quantify it onscreen. Their user-friendly design falls in line with the general trend toward the consumerization of IT, the purpose of which is to facilitate technology adoption by all. In this instance, the goal is to eliminate technical barriers between decision makers and complex data sets, so executive dashboards tend to be relatively user friendly, regardless of where decision makers may fall along the digital fluency spectrum.

"The digital fluency spectrum" – Leadership 009

Things only get more exciting from here.

Moving beyond executive dashboards, cognitive computing and natural language AI interfaces like IBM's Watson and Google's Deep Mind soon will help executives create predictive models using voice commands and natural language. These are the same types of models we mentioned earlier—the ones that explore possible outcomes and scenarios, and test hypothetical decisions. What this means is that decision makers soon will have access to smart dashboards and cloud-based deep learning computers equipped with natural language interfaces that will essentially function as advisors.

This capability is giving rise to an ecosystem of intelligent recommendation systems that leverage Big Data, machine learning and predictive analytics to help decision makers analyze and understand data and model outcomes, and recommend the best possible courses of action.

Five years from now, advanced digital decision-making tools will give their users a significant edge over decision makers who still use outdated analysis and practices. If these tools are not on your radar already, they should be.

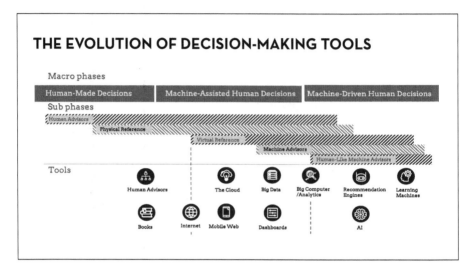

Leadership 010

HOW CIOS AND CTOS CAN BECOME FUTURE-PROOFING CHAMPIONS

In addition to their other responsibilities, CIOs and CTOs should provide senior executives and decision makers with adequate training and resources to ensure their fluency regarding new technologies. This means that CIOs and CTOs should be, at least in part, responsible for the direction and implementation of digital transformation strategies and milestones across the organization, and for that of their fellow executives by way of training and skill building.

Ensuring the technological fluency of senior executives is vital to the success of digital transformation. It cannot be treated as an afterthought or a secondary objective, or left to chance. It also cannot be brushed aside by decision makers who would prefer to delegate technological fluency to subordinates and surrogates. Decision makers, whether they are CEOs or board members, cannot be the least informed and the least technologically capable members of their organizations. Not anymore. Failure to connect executives with the technology ecosystems built specifically to improve outcomes will only result in chronic failures of leadership, digital transformation and futureproofing.

A technology-driven culture cannot be effectively built and fostered in an organization whose leadership does not fully embrace technology and its value. This is particularly true of the CEO. Beyond the practical aspects of ensuring that decision makers take full advantage of these technologies, no organization can be fully engaged in digital transformation and data-driven decision making if the CEO does not behave as the chief evangelist for change.

Leaders set priorities and lead by example. What is personally important to them always trickles down across their organizations. What is not does not, and there is no getting around that.

LAYERING TECHNOLOGY-BASED LEADERSHIP

It is important to note that data-driven decision models operate in layers. At every level of an organization where someone has a decision to make about a course of action, timely access to relevant and accurate data can make all the difference. Sales and business development representatives need access to data that is relevant to their tasks and objectives. Customer service representatives need access to data that is relevant to the cases they are working on. Product development teams, marketing teams, content developers, web and mobile UX developers, business analysts, accounts receivable coordinators, facility managers, recruiters, and HR managers—everyone needs access to pertinent data to leverage in real time.

The bird's-eye view is that data-powered software solutions should be deployed across the organization. Every function at every level requires a dashboard and some manner of software that caters to each employee's function. For instance, product managers need data to gauge the effectiveness of their product's market performance, as well as identify obstacles, anticipate possible problems, and look for new or otherwise tangential opportunities for improvement. This includes a host of data including sales figures, order history, inventory

breakdowns, supply chain data, returns, customer feedback, and demographic breakdowns of likely versus actual users.
Thanks to the proliferation of IoT and sensors, new categories of data points can now be monitored and leveraged by product managers. Product usage is one example. Where and how is the product being used? How long is it being used? How often is it being used? Is the product functioning properly or prone to crashes or errors? All this information can be compiled into on-demand reports and management dashboards.

With sales data, product teams can make real-time adjustments to product price points. They can accelerate or slow down production. Based on where orders are coming from, product teams can prioritize shipments and optimize their logistics. Based on how many complaints or customer support calls the company is getting about the product, they can assign adequate customer support resources to address customer needs. They can decide to create content and update their FAQs to help educate users and improve their ability to troubleshoot on their own. With feedback from users and retailers, they also can identify areas of improvement for the next iteration of the product, from performance and design features to packaging and pricing.

Everything that can be measured can be quantified, and everything that can quantified can be improved. Pricing, packaging, sales, features, UX, delivery, customer support—every detail that ultimately contributes to the success of a product's performance— can be measured and applied to making decisions that will drive improvements and consistent positive outcomes.

None of this would be possible without access to pertinent data. Product management teams would be flying blind, or at least they would still rely on customer surveys, anecdotal information, and pure instinct to make critical decisions and timely course corrections. This is the power of data-driven design, and it scales to every corner and layer of the organization, from the receptionist greeting prospective clients in the lobby to the CEO and board of directors contemplating their company's next series of bold strategic moves.

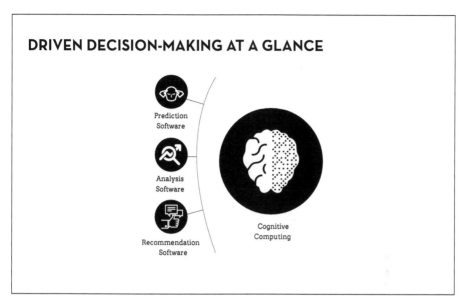

DRIVEN DECISION-MAKING AT A GLANCE

Prediction Software

Analysis Software

Recommendation Software

Cognitive Computing

Leadership 011

DATA-DRIVEN LEADERSHIP IS ENHANCED LEADERSHIP

The idea behind data-driven leadership, then, is to use advanced data analysis tools, predictive modeling software, and recommendation systems to enhance decision makers' situational awareness, as well as magnify their knowledge and help close the probability gap between guessing and knowing.

For the sake of clarity, we have broken this down into simple quadrants that should help visualize how to build a 360-degree data-driven decision-making ecosystem. It addresses four critical functions of the ecosystem: awareness, adaptability, agility, and measurement. Because we are dealing with technologies that significantly enhance these four functions, we will address the quadrants as hyper-awareness, hyper-adaptability, hyper-agility, and hyper-measurement.

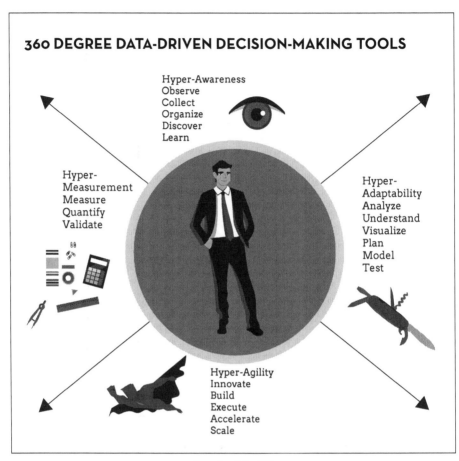

360 DEGREE DATA-DRIVEN DECISION-MAKING TOOLS

Hyper-Awareness
Observe
Collect
Organize
Discover
Learn

Hyper-
Measurement
Measure
Quantify
Validate

Hyper-
Adaptability
Analyze
Understand
Visualize
Plan
Model
Test

Hyper-Agility
Innovate
Build
Execute
Accelerate
Scale

Leadership 012

Hyper-awareness focuses on the ability to identify and anticipate shifts, trends, opportunities, threats, problems, potential partners, and every other kind of factor that could, in some way, affect the outcome of a decision. Hyper-awareness combines observation and situational awareness regarding everything from sales and production to employee morale and retail foot traffic with market data, social data, industry news, analyst predictions, investor feedback, and so on. Think of it as a control room for all the data in the world that could be relevant to the organization. This also includes data and news that may not be on the decision maker's radar, but should be.

This aspect of the quadrant is about discovery, data collection and sorting. It is Big Data applied to a 360-degree view of the organization's internal and external universe. Management dashboards tend to address this function, although the breadth of information they provide should be significantly broadened. The injection of AI should help cast a wider net and identify bits of information and business intelligence that have traditionally remained beyond the scope of traditional dashboards or were deemed too small or remote to matter. In the information age, no bit of data is too small or remote to matter. Every customer complaint can be noted and addressed, as can every consumer recommendation regarding product design, delivery speed, website UX, and price.

Hyper-adaptability focuses on the ability to analyze and understand that data, then make appropriate course adjustments where applicable. Hyper-adaptability relies on machine learning and low-level algorithms to identify patterns, trends and hidden connections in large sets of data. This process of analysis and pattern recognition organizes its findings and alerts decision makers about potential opportunities, problems, market shifts, and changing economic conditions. It provides a layer of insight that functions as a catalyst for response and a vehicle for short- and long-term adaptation to shifting market needs. As cognitive computing and AI bring more functionality to this analysis and insights layer, we see the function shifting from mere delivery to actual recommendation. Increasingly, this part of the data-driven decision-making technology quadrant shifts from simply telling decision makers about the data to advising them what to do with it.

Hyper-agility refers to the ability to accelerate innovation, deploy new technology solutions, explore new business models, test ideas and scenarios virtually, and inject consistent success with velocity and scale. This is the part of the quadrant where knowledge and analysis are turned into action. It is the rubber-meets-the-road aspect of data-driven leadership. Up to this point, technology's role was to inform and recommend. Now technology's role is to help organizations execute and bring about the desired outcomes we have been discussing until now. This includes, but certainly isn't limited to, advanced project management tools, intuitive productivity tools, gamification, self-correcting pricing algorithms, smart manufacturing (Industrial IoT—

IIoT), chatbots, augmented reality, design virtualization, 3D printing, mobile solutions, remote working solutions, smart automation, and AI. Beyond technology, whose purpose is to facilitate and accelerate a company's ability to move with speed and precision toward its intended goals, hyper-agility also requires a culture and operational framework designed to eliminate obstacles to agility. As data-driven decision making and leadership scales across the organization, doers tend to be better equipped to self manage and complete tasks on time. When human failures occur, hyper-agile organizations have mechanisms in place to self correct. For instance, automation features in advanced project management tools are designed to prompt team members who may be deemed at risk of falling behind schedule to prioritize task and assign additional resources to complete that individual's secondary tasks. Expectations and training tend to change as data-driven organizations become increasingly agile. Agility can be taught, just like any other skill. But agile companies don't just equip workers with tools to improve their agility and efficiency, they also equip them with training, operational guidelines, and a culture that fosters and rewards fluency in problem solving.

Note that without data-driven leaders guiding their organization through a digital transformation process, no company can or will achieve this degree of operational efficiency. Without it, the stated objective of consistently improving outcomes will not be achieved.

Hyper-measurement refers to the ability to measure and quantify performance at scale. The outcome of every activity must be measured and quantified for decision makers to gauge their effectiveness. The reactions and ripple effects of every decision also should be measured to gauge their impact across a wide variety of data sets. Mapping these fields of cause and effect help decision makers and the learning machines they work with to understand, visualize and interpret the effectiveness of their decisions.

This function helps decision makers not only analyze and understand what works and why (or what doesn't work and why), but also fine tune their decision making, make timely course corrections and work toward constantly improving outcomes over time. This kind of decision-making leadership cannot exist outside of a data-driven measurement culture. The two are indivisible.

WHAT ARE EXAMPLES OF KEY OUTCOMES THAT RESULT FROM DATA-DRIVEN LEADERSHIP?

At the executive level, key potential outcomes of data-driven leadership include:

- Accelerating innovation,
- Identifying and quantifying potential market opportunities,
- Identifying and contextualizing potential threats,
- Improving overall organizational adaptability and agility,
- Reducing risk,
- Anticipating and reacting to market disruption,
- Improving digital and technical adaptation,
- Shifting from reactive to proactive models of adaptation and industry disruption,
- Identifying technical inflection points internally and in the market,
- Validating potential partnerships and acquisitions,
- Modeling and testing strategic plans virtually,
- Identifying problem areas within the organization, and
- Course-correcting in real time.

At the LoB level, key objectives of data-driven leadership include:

- Accelerating and improving product design,
- Improving the effectiveness of marketing spend,
- Improving customer experiences across all channels,
- Improving customer relationships, particularly in regards to

retention, loyalty and buy rate,

- Using predictive modeling to optimize outcomes,

- Improving the accuracy of campaign and employee performance metrics,

- Improving employee retention,

- Consistently identifying and recruiting top industry talent,

- Accelerating customer service ticket resolutions,

- Improving cost efficiency,

- Improving production and coordination efficiency,

- Improving workplace safety,

- Improving productivity and facilitating collaboration across the organization,

- Accelerating internal training and skill building, and

- Boosting employee morale.

Note how well the items on both of these lists fit into our overall futureproofing model.

Let's look at how this kind of model can drive positive outcomes and necessary change in the real world, even when companies already put technology at the heart of their business.

Hopefully, you read or re-read Building Dragons before picking up Futureproof. If you have, you will remember the chapter in which we outlined how Disney leveraged technology (sensors, Cloud, AI) to create and deliver magical experiences. We aren't going to revisit that. Instead, let's talk about one major change that Disney made internally that had a huge impact on its operations, capabilities and overall agility. It created a massive DevOps program.

Disney had done everything right. It had invested heavily in technology, created a flat structure, assigned resources everywhere it needed to, even allowed every division and business to have its own

CTO. On many levels, this was a good thing. Every group, team and unit could operate independently of the rest of the organization and handle its own technology needs on its own. This model was operationally agile, and it enabled Disney to operate efficiently and fast. But that much autonomy also meant fragmentation of IT. Fragmentation of IT on a scale that, with a company as large as Disney, created an entirely new and serious challenge: How do you get all of those CTOs to talk to each other and collaborate at scale? How do you get all of your systems to work well together? How do you move the company forward at the same pace?

To help solve that problem, Disney adopted a shadow IT strategy. It started building a DevOps model (a hybrid of software development and operations). DevOps is kind of like a special operations role for IT.

After building the model, Disney set out to deploy it across the entire organization, one business unit and division at a time. This proved to be a practical challenge in regard to technology, processes, competencies, and the scale of the endeavor. It was also a cultural challenge. The DevOps project team had to contend with fiefdoms and silos, politics and distrust, and skepticism and resistance, but, ultimately, one win at a time, one proof of concept at a time, the DevOps model began to take root.

Let's talk results. While not obvious to the general public, the impact was massive. With the introduction of DevOps, every process and system in Disney's technology stack started getting more streamlined and efficient, from point of sale terminals to the cloud hosting of content. At the parks, daily processes that used to take multiple employees hours to manage were shortened to 30 minutes. Problems that used to take ride engineers weeks to solve ahead of a launch now only took a few days.

Broken down into broader themes, Disney's adoption of Shadow IT and its introduction of DevOps improved three key areas:

1. *Velocity: Engineering and business units are now better able to adapt, solve problems, design solutions, and improve processes at a pace that matches their real world needs.*

2. *Scale: Disney learned to better manage its ever-expanding*

technology stack. What had begun to feel unmanageable is under control again. Not only does this free up resources and allow Disney's technology infrastructure to run smoothly, it also removes obstacles to the stack's inevitable next series of evolutions and growth. Disney would have been stuck in place had the problem of scale not been solved.

3. *Reliability: Before the DevOps program, systems weren't uniformly configured, causing inconsistency in performance, latency and a litany of problems that made Disney technology infrastructure unruly. With the introduction of configuration management across the organization, Disney was able to make its IT stack much more efficient, predictable and reliable.*

PUTTING TECHNOLOGY AT THE HEART OF YOUR BUSINESS

The trick with writing too specifically about technology in a book like this one is that technology changes fast. Too fast. Tools we write about here may be obsolete by the time this book finds you. We can take a few chances here and there, but, overall, it's best to focus on trends and the type of advice that will still be useful five, six, seven, maybe even 10 years from now. A lot can change between now and 2025. A lot will. But fundamental lessons and insights into futureproofing won't.

What matters most is that futureproof companies all learn to become technology companies somewhere along the way. It doesn't matter if they're airlines, banks, hotels, public utilities, restaurant chains, or law firms, tech is the future. Except for the odd analog mom and pop shop that bucks every convention because it can, the other 99.999999999 percent of companies don't have a choice here. Either they become technology companies or they don't. And, if they don't, they won't be able to compete in a technology-driven market. What happened to bookstores and video rental chains will eventually happen to every other industry. It doesn't take special glasses to see what is happening to brick-and-mortar retailers. Healthcare is on the edge of a radical transformation thanks to mobility, the cloud and the IoT. The auto industry is about to completely reinvent itself. Smart infrastructure (smart cities, smart manufacturing, autonomous vehicles, self-managing systems) is already starting to spread. Everything is changing. No business will be spared.

We have reached an inflection point. This tsunami of disruption isn't coming, it's already here. It's *adapt or die* time. To get through this, every organization is going to have to start getting elbow deep in technology solutions. That means reading the tech industry press, visiting vendors, scheduling demos, speaking with consultants and analysts, hiring technologists, attending product launches (virtually, even), and testing every new product that even remotely sounds like it might be useful. Every manager and leader should spend at least half an hour a day looking for the next digital tool or technology solution that will solve a problem for them, improve a process or create a new opportunity.

Senior leaders, especially CEOs, COOs, CIOs, and CTOs, should take a page from the Ally playbook and pay attention to where tech-focused venture capitalists are putting their money. What technologies and companies are they backing and why? Everyone should be paying attention to where developers, executives and designers go when they leave innovation giants like Google, Amazon, Uber, Microsoft, and Apple. What enticed them to leave? What are they working on now? Which tech companies are forming unlikely alliances? Which products and services companies are crossing over into new markets? What role do new technologies, or new applications of familiar technologies, play in these changes?

IT leaders should be nothing short of obsessive about AI breakthroughs, mixed reality milestones, IoT advancements, and hot new entrants in productivity, collaboration, and analytics tools. Every ripple in data security news, every rumor of a new blockchain application, every hint of progress in human-machine partnership should lead to a fact-finding mission.

If it has to start with senior executives reading *TechCrunch, Wired, MIT Technology Review, CNet, Recode,* and *Fast Company,* alongside the *Wall Street Journal* every morning, then so be it. It has to start somewhere. Technology is becoming the beating heart of business. So, if you want to build a futureproof company, you are going to have to become passionate about technology.

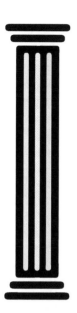

CHAPTER 7:
CULTURE

"Culture eats strategy for breakfast." – Peter Drucker

THE NEW FUNDAMENTALS OF CULTURE

Leadership is great, hiring and nurturing awesome people is too, but putting them all in a room together will only get you so far. In the end, *culture* appears to be the real X-Factor behind the success of the world's greatest companies. When you look at companies like Disney, Apple, Zappos, Starbucks, and LEGO, it's culture you notice first. It's culture that drives success.

Culture can manifest itself in a variety of forms. It is generally *layered* rather than monolithic. What we mean is that a company culture isn't just one thing. Regardless of what you may have read or heard, there's no discernable "Disney culture," "Starbucks culture" or "Apple culture." Hide the company's identity and break down its culture into a bullet list, and you won't be able to tell one tech company, hotel chain or media company from another. Culture is a layered construct. There are cultures of outstanding customer service, which we find at Disney and Starbucks, and cultures of gorgeous industrial design, which we find at Apple and BMW, and cultures of innovation, which we find at Tesla and Qualcomm. And, to a great extent, cultures of outstanding customer service, gorgeous industrial design, and innovation can be found at all of the aforementioned companies and countless others. When you break it down, culture is a layer cake of values, purpose and priorities. Look at any successful company today and you are likely to find that their "culture" is really an amalgam of priorities and choices that have been, over time, deliberately baked into their overall brand strategy and day-to-day operations. That's how companies like Starbucks and Disney can be known for their customer service cultures, their cultures of innovation *and* their cultures of employee engagement.

At one point, these companies decided that they would make big bets on innovation and developed innovation-driving capabilities. Over time, these capabilities and resources proved themselves valuable, and cemented their importance in the company's key strategic decisions and daily operations. They may have assigned a chief innovation officer to help drive innovation across the organization, for instance. They may have invested in a massive R&D program. They may have hired a small army of engineers and patent attorneys to look for and identify valuable IP to be leveraged into their product and service offerings by way of licensing and slick integration. Once these investments were made, the resources tasked with making good on those bets got to work justifying their funding. Those that were successful in doing so, and proved the value of innovation, got more funding. They made more bets, bigger bets and built on every subsequent success. Little by little, innovation became an integral part of those companies because innovation paid off. Thus, a culture of innovation was born.

Let's go back to our layer cake of values, purpose and priorities:

- What kind of company do we want to be?

- What are we here to do?

- What do we need to focus on?

That's the recipe for culture building.

What kind of company do we want to be can be translated into *what do we want to be known for?* Magical experiences? Outstanding customer service? The coolest tech gadgets? The fastest cars? The most reliable tires? The fastest coast-to-coast flights? The cheapest hotel prices? The best damn latte anywhere? Pain-free banking? The lowest employee turnover in our industry? Double-digit growth YoY? The most beautiful designs? The most comfortable beds? The most authentic burgers? The most competent surgical staff in the country? The best education money can buy? The best graphics and storytelling in the industry? A perfect custom fit every time? The most diverse company in the industry? The list could go on forever. That part of culture-building boils down to what your value proposition, as a company and as a brand, needs to be. There's no also-in when it comes to that aspect of culture. "We build widgets used in other widgets" doesn't build a foundation for culture. It just frames your company into a common stereotype: Widgets, you say? Insert generic industrial/manufacturing stereotype. "We sell insurance." Oh? Insert generic insurance sales stereotype. That isn't culture. It's a cliché. "We make the SOCs that go into 80 percent of the world's smart drones," however, carries more weight. "We sell data breach insurance to all of the world's major retailers" also goes a long way toward defining a company's identity and, consequently, its value.

More often than not, this begins with a choice to either be the best or biggest at something, then pick what that something is, and, once that's done, find the next thing that can be added to it. For instance, the following list would provide the company behind each item a very specific target.

- The biggest supplier of IoT processors in the world.

- The makers of the world's most delicious strawberry sorbet.

- The best Italian restaurant in New York City.

- The makers of the best electric luxury car in the world.

- The fastest growing social network in the world.

- The most reliable source of fact-checked news.

- The world's most transparent and ethical Fortune 500 company.

Once that's done, what comes next?

- The most culturally diverse company in the industry.

- The most environmentally sustainable company in the U.S.

- The best and slickest integration of AI in the customer experience.

- The first company of its kind to be 100 percent cruelty free.

- Voted one of the world's best places to work for nine years in a row.

- Consistently two years ahead of the competition in performance and design.

- The first company to effectively crack the mobile workplace and flex-time code.

What kind of company do we want to be? It isn't a question you ask just once. It's a question you have to ask regularly, along with *are we the company we said we wanted to be* and *now that we are, how can we build on that?*

What are we here to do is a little less vision oriented and more purpose driven. In a way, it's more pragmatic and tactical. *We're here to be profitable. We're here to increase our market share. We're here to become a leader in our industry.* You have to start somewhere there too. But what is a company, any company, *really* there to do beyond obvious Business 101 objectives? Companies with strong, effective cultures tend to be built on a unique set of answers to that question.

Do you think that Tesla's list of answers to *"what are we here to do?"* is going to look like Toyota's or GM's? Do you think that Amazon's list of answers is going to look like Walmart's or Sears'? Companies with the kinds of cultures that drive growth, innovation and success tend to find specific answers to that question.

- We're here to create universal compatibility standards between all devices in the IoT.

- We're here to build the most innovative company in the world.

- We're here to help farmers solve all of their climate change-related challenges.

- We're here to make smart homes affordable for everyone.

- We're here to make telemedicine so userfriendly that even the most technology-averse patients will have no trouble navigating it.

- We're here to make online banking 100 percent safe from hackers and cyber attacks.

- We're here to make mobile collaboration work the way it's supposed to work.

- We're here to bring proper, authentic, Vietnamese street food to hundreds of cities around the world.

- We're here to build the most culturally-diverse workforce on the planet.

- We're here to designbuild the smart, energy-efficient cities of the future.

Specificity of purpose matters. It isn't just a component of culture development. It is, at its core, a valuable strategic exercise—a business imperative, really. It just so happens that companies that take the time to think about this, to crystallize and articulate their purpose, also tend to create cultures that drive that purpose (or rather, that set of combined purposes, since there is rarely just one).

Clarity of vision has to be followed by clarity of purpose. It's the same for companies as it is for people. Have you ever met someone who naturally exuded confidence, competence and purpose? Someone whose identity, at least in the way that if formed in your mind, was built upon these attributes? Someone with a sense of purpose isn't lost or adrift. Someone with a sense of purpose knows exactly who they are, what they are there to do and what drives them forward. They know how to define success and what resources to invest in to achieve it. They are driven by this. Companies are no different. A culture of one is, at its core, not that different from a culture of many. Companies that know what they want to be known for, what they want to accomplish, what they are generally about, naturally build cultures that support their sense of purpose and drive the pursuit of that purpose.

What do we need to focus on? More often than not, there is a time factor associated with that question. What do we need to focus on *first?* What do we need to focus on *right now?* What do we need to focus on *next?* This part is about execution.

- How do we prioritize?

- How do we invest?

- How do we plan for the next phases of this?

- How do we build mechanisms in support of this?

The question comes down to prioritization first because most companies are likely to have a limited amount of resources (Bandwidth, infrastructure, leadership, skillsets, and so on) at any given time.

- What is most important now?

- What do we also need to start working on right now, given how long it will take to rampup or build?

Those initiatives could be focused on building something new, improving a program that is already delivering results, reviving a stalled program, or solving a failing business practice.

Examples:

> *Building something new:* Investing in AR and the IoT to redesign our in-store retail experiences to increase foot traffic, unique visitors, average purchase value, customer loyalty, and positive word-of-mouth.

> *Improving a program that is already delivering results:* Improving the speed and user friendliness of our mobile and omnichannel shopping ecosystem to increase product discovery, app downloads and purchases.

Reviving a stalled program: Our customer loyalty program was off to a great start, but it's hit a plateau this past quarter. How do we get it going again?

Solving a failing business practice: Our customer-facing employee turnover is way too high. What can we do to improve retention?

By prioritizing, companies effectively choose what their cultural imperatives will be. Will innovation be prioritized over customer service? Will low pricing be prioritized over fast home delivery? Will operational efficiency be prioritized over employee retention? And so on. What they decide to focus on (or not focus on) will inform what they will be best known for.

For some companies, culture will focus on some combination of innovation, design, amazing customer experiences, market leadership, operational agility, employee loyalty, and exemplary leadership, for instance. In many cases, however, culture will be shaped by some combination of ineffective management, risk-averse leadership, poor customer service, botched marketing campaigns, uninspired acquisitions, eroding market share, product recalls, workplace discrimination scandals, and lack of vision.

Culture, at its core, is born out of decisions about what is most important. These decisions exist along three overlapping but distinct dimensions: Values, purpose and priorities.

This teaches us that culture doesn't have a chicken or egg problem. Great company cultures are the product of inspired leadership long before they scale. They then take root and grow across organizations when people, united by a common vision and purpose, breathe more life into them, nurture them and weave them into their business practices. Great cultures tend to also spread from inside organizations to their customers. We see this with Apple fans, LEGO collectors and Tesla owners. Consumer goods companies with strong cultures naturally build tribes, inside and outside their walls. B2B companies do the same, though perhaps with more subtle expressions of admiration and loyalty than their B2C counterparts. Military branches, universities, religious denominations, athletic communities, political groups, and every other organization you can think of has its own unique culture...

All tribes are held together and ultimately defined by their cultures. Once in place, great company cultures tend to feed their own lifecycles. By virtue of the fact that they already exist, work and influence values, purpose and priorities, they, in turn, help shape generations of leaders, employees and customers and tend to become self perpetuating. So what does the culture lifecycle look like?

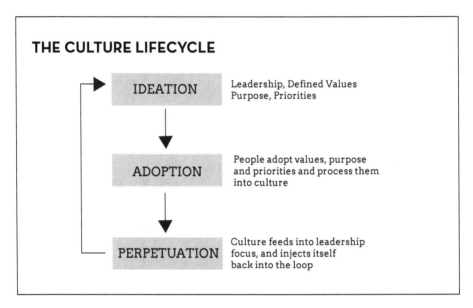

For companies to develop and build strong, consistent, lasting cultures, they need three crucial elements, all of which happen to be fundamental pillars of dragon building and futureproofing, at their core—leadership, people and, as they move forward, culture itself, as a self-reinforcing and self-perpetuating mechanism.

OTHER TANGIBLE DIMENSIONS OF CULTURE

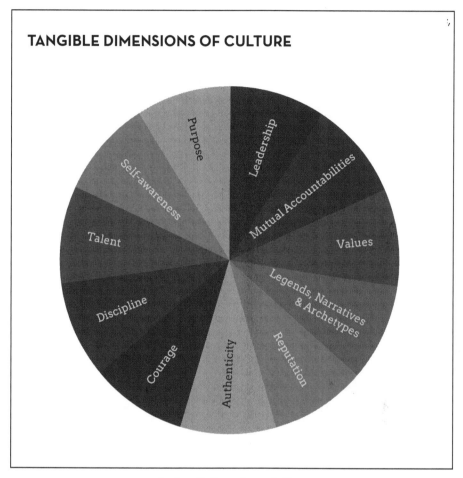

TANGIBLE DIMENSIONS OF CULTURE

Authenticity and reputation.

Other vital aspects or "dimensions" of culture that we find at success-ful, agile and adaptable companies are:

- Mutual accountability,

- Legends, narratives, and archetypes,

- Self-awareness,

- Talent,

- Discipline,

- Courage,

- Authenticity, and

- Reputation.

Let's break these down:

Mutual accountability - Mutual accountability is one of the most basic and crucial components of any successful team. It doesn't matter if it's a team of two or a team of 5,000. As long as people are accountable to each other, they will get the job done properly. Mutual accountability is different from being accountable to a "boss" in the sense that the job to be done doesn't lead to a punishment or reward outcome, but rather, constant social validation within the group. The same mechanisms that fuel peer pressure also fuel accountability to your peers. Why? Because as uncomfortable and stressful as it may be to have your boss disapprove of you, it's a lot more uncomfortable and stressful to be rejected by your peer group. Look at any cohesive unit, whether in the military or in a corporate setting, and what separates a high-performing unit from a low-performing unit is the extent to which that unit's members are held accountable to one another. When you build a culture of mutual accountability, you build a culture of cohesion and collaboration. That kind of culture doesn't require boss walking around, cracking a whip.

Legends, narratives and archetypes - Legends also are common in successful business cultures. Stories give meaning, right? Stories create structure for value systems. Who is the hero? Why is the hero the hero? How do we, as a group, define success? What values do we cherish? Stories help us frame value systems and identify behavioral ideals. They set the stage and pave the way for what must naturally come next.

Think about the legends around billion-dollar companies that were started in a garage, for instance: Jeff Bezos and Amazon. Steve Jobs and Apple. Heck, the entire tech industry started in a garage, didn't it? As the story goes, Dave Packard and Bill Hewlett formed their company out of a garage at 367 Addison Ave., in Palo Alto, California, in 1939.

Their capital at the time was $538. HP's first product was built in that garage. It wasn't a computer though. It was an audio oscillator. One of HP's first customers was Walt Disney Studios, which, at the time, was looking to push moviegoing experiences with the release of *Fantasia*, the first major film to be released in stereo.

Think about the legend being created here. Think about the impact a story like this would have on HP employees. Two Stanford grads at the eve of World War 2 started out with a few hundred bucks and a dusty garage, helped Disney make history and built their company into a tech giant raking in tens of billions of dollars in revenue all around the world. Think about the can-do attitude this kind of legend would naturally inject into the company's culture. Think about the spirit of entrepreneurialism it would bake into every project team's leadership, the work ethic, the mystique of elegant problem-solving and the make-it-work approach to every task. Imagine being on the receiving end of a friendly but firm pep talk along the lines of *"this company was built by two guys in a garage working without computers and virtually no budget. Tell me again what your project's hang up is?"* Legends always set the stage for company cultures, for better and for worse.

Adaptability - We can look at adaptability and agility together. Adaptability is the trait that makes people and companies resilient in the face of challenges and change. Adaptability is the ability for a company to, for instance, abandon a dying business model and replace it with a new one. You may remember how, in its early days, Netflix shifted from shipping DVDs straight to consumers to streaming content. Why? Because the powers that be at Netflix realized that if they didn't make that change, if they didn't adapt to new technology breakthroughs, Netflix would die, so Netflix adapted and survived, even thrived. Few business examples of adaptability resonate with us more than what happened with Netflix and Blockbuster between 2000 and 2010: Blockbuster, the incumbent movie rental company, failed to invest in new technologies, failed to adapt to changing market conditions, and that was that. Netflix, the challenger, adapted to changing market conditions, made the right technology bets and became the world's 10th biggest internet company (as of the drafting of this book anyway), with billions in annual revenue.

While "survival of the fittest" is both a scientific fact *and* a common cliché used to explain why some individuals, species, organizations, cultures, and civilizations endure or die, "survival of the most adaptable" is actually a more accurate insight into the matter. "Fitness" is overrated in a rapidly changing environment. Fitness can only protect you from so much disruption. Adaptability, however, is what usually gives companies the ability to navigate change and disruption, and either survive or thrive as a result of that change. In an era of constant and rapid change, the most adaptable companies will always have a definitive advantage over their less adaptable counterparts. In terms of culture, adaptability manifests itself as the ability to see change coming, break down that change into threats and opportunities, then refocus objectives, reassign resources in support of those objectives, retool, retrain, and adjust course. At its simplest, an organization will barely feel the change at all. It may even feel incremental, like replacing aging video conferencing equipment with more up-to-date technology. At its most challenging, a company may have to divest itself of once vital business units, reorganize its management structure and revamp its business model. IBM and Qualcomm's business evolutions over the years are good examples of the operationalization of this trait in action.

Agility - When we speak about agility, we address the speed and relative ease with which an organization can adapt to change. The more agile a company, the less friction gets in the way of its adaptation. Companies with strong change management cultures, for instance, tend to be operationally more agile than companies with traditional "but we've always done things this way" cultures.

One thing we keep running into in our dealings with companies big and small, old and young, is that the more "digital" a company is, or in a sense, the more virtual it is, the more agile it tends to be. Part of the reason for this is that companies that rely heavily on digital tools to run their day-to-day operations tend to be less tethered to technology and infrastructure investments. If one app or technology solution doesn't work as well as it was supposed to, it isn't that complicated to switch to another one. Course corrections may be as simple as downloading a new app onto employee-operated devices. Worst case scenario, databases might have to migrate, but most of the change happens in the digital space, not in the physical world. And the less physical weight has to be pushed, the easier it is to push. The lesson here being that the more digital and tech literate a company is, the more agile that company tends to be when the time comes to adapt to change and disruption.

Self-awareness - Self-awareness is conceptually one of the simplest traits to explain, but one of the most challenging to operationalize. In the spirit of keeping things simple, self-awareness in a business culture context can best be explained as knowing who you are as a company and being conscious of how true to that identity your actions, as a company, are. For instance, a company that is self-aware will simultaneously market itself as being committed to workplace diversity and operationalize that focus by hiring, developing and investing in a diverse workforce. The gap between identity and action will be zero (or as close to zero as can be expected). A company that is not self-aware, on the other hand, will market itself as being committed to workplace diversity, but will fall short of operationalizing that focus. While it may talk a good game, the majority of its hires may be white, the majority of its senior leadership may be male and its internal HR policies may even provide cover for rampant sexual harassment. The bigger the gap between a company's stated identity and the articulation of that identity in the real world, the less self-aware it is.

A common behavior of companies with low self-awareness is a public and internal denial of facts pertaining to that gap. A company with low self-awareness may, for instance, only realize that it fell short of delivering on its promise of diversity and inclusion once a scandal erupts that casts a light on its failures in that regard. Once the scandal occurs, the company may then acknowledge the problem, pledge to correct it and set out to do so in earnest. Other companies with little to no self-awareness confronted with a similar problem may instead deny that they have failed and hold on to the notion that they don't need to course correct at all.

Self-awareness is not limited to workforce diversity. It can be applied to just about anything, from fair trade practices and ethics to technology adoption and innovation. Companies that realize they have fallen behind in technology adoption when they indeed have are self-aware. Companies that have fallen behind in technology adoption but refuse to acknowledge it (and do what they need to do about it) are not. Self-awareness, as a cultural trait, is therefore vital to the survival of companies and organizations that hope to survive and thrive through periods of disruption and change. The more self-aware an organization is, the better equipped it will be to realistically and effectively evaluate opportunities and threats and gauge its successes and failures in regard to how well it addresses them. Self-aware company cultures are generally good at change management. Company cultures with little self-awareness—company cultures of denial, basically—tend to not fare well at all in periods of disruption and change.

Talent - We've all heard that hard work beats talent, and it's true, but why choose hard work over talent when you can have both? Hard work is vital to success, but talent is a force-multiplier. Think about where we would be without talented researchers and innovators, creatives, communicators, and decision-makers. Talent may only add 2 percent genius to a business recipe of 49 percent hard work and 49% percent, but it's that 2 percent that might make the difference between success and failure. Where would Apple, Tesla, Oakley, Lego, Adidas, Qualcomm, Microsoft, GE, Sony, and Netflix be without design engineering, marketing, salesmanship, or political talent?

Companies that invest in talent, not merely "headcount" (or more colloquially "asses in seats") tend to fare better in times of disruption and change than companies that obsess over workforce productivity and optimization at the expense of innovation, problem solving and entrepreneurial mindsets. Figuring out how to do something better, then doing it better, is at least as valuable as working hard at solving a problem. You might be tempted to argue that it may be even more important. "Work smarter, not harder," right? Maybe in some cases. Again, the beauty of crafting high performing organizational cultures is that you don't have to pick one or the other. You can invest in both. In fact, you should. That is why companies that are good at identifying, investing in, developing, and nurturing talent alongside hard work and solid work ethics tend to be better equipped to deal with disruption and change than companies that treat talent as an afterthought or a magic bullet.

Discipline - Discipline is the flip side of that coin. It fits into the work ethic piece of that equation. Discipline is predictable, dependable and reliable. Discipline is why you show up, give it your all, don't quit when things get difficult, and don't panic when things go sideways. Discipline is what separates amateurs from professionals. Without discipline, there can be no practical expertise, professional responsibility, continuous learning, or improvement. The greatest talent in the world, even paired with the most brilliant idea in the world, will be wasted without discipline. The hard truth about discipline, though, is that it is a cultural trait. Military organizations are perfect examples of how discipline is baked into organizational cultures, and how discipline impacts competence and effectiveness. Study any military unit in the world and you will find a direct correlation between discipline and effectiveness. Units that are 100 percent squared away perform like well-oiled machines. Conversely, units that are undisciplined are sloppy in their execution, unreliable and far less effective than their disciplined counterparts.

Consider the difference between a disciplined commercial airline pilot and an undisciplined airline pilot, for instance, and the impact this may have on the safety of his passengers.

Consider the difference between a disciplined customer service representative and an undisciplined customer service representative, and the impact this may have on the experience of customers looking for assistance or redress.

Consider the difference between a disciplined web developer, project manager or marketing director and an undisciplined web developer, project manager or marketing director and the impact they may have on hitting critical deadlines and maintaining high quality standards.

Discipline isn't just an individual trait that people either have or don't have. Discipline is taught. Discipline is enforced. Discipline can and must be baked into a company's culture for that organization to perform, evolve and change evenly and with minimal internal friction. We aren't suggesting that you run your business like a military boot camp. Far from it. What we are suggesting though, is that you learn the importance of building discipline into your business model from the military and bake it into your company culture. One good place to start is to recruit veterans and individual with military experience,

11"Adm. McRaven Urges Graduates to Find Courage to Change the World." *UT News*, 16 May 2014, news.utexas.edu/2014/05/16/mcraven-urges-graduates-to-find-courage-to-change-the-world.

particularly to work in parts of your business that are disorganized, underperforming or resistant to change.

Here's a lesson that Admiral William H. McRaven, 9th commander of U.S. Special Operations Command and a Navy SEAL likes to share [11] about discipline and the impact of discipline on professional effectiveness:

> *"Every morning in basic SEAL training, my instructors, who at the time were all Vietnam veterans, would show up in my barracks room and the first thing they would inspect was your bed. If you did it right, the corners would be square, the covers pulled tight, the pillow centered just under the headboard and the extra blanket folded neatly at the foot of the rack—that's Navy talk for bed.*
>
> *"It was a simple task—mundane at best. But every morning we were required to make our bed to perfection. It seemed a little ridiculous at the time, particularly in light of the fact that we were aspiring to be real warriors, tough battle-hardened SEALs, but the wisdom of this simple act has been proven to me many times over.*
>
> *"If you make your bed every morning you will have accomplished the first task of the day. It will give you a small sense of pride, and it will encourage you to do another task and another and another. By the end of the day, that one task completed will have turned into many tasks completed. Making your bed will also reinforce the fact that little things in life matter. If you can't do the little things right, you will never do the big things right."*

That lesson is true, regardless of the organization: Discipline matters. Not because of an abstract belief that discipline and organization go hand-in-hand, but because discipline is a fundamental trait of successful and driven people, and disciplined, successful, driven people create cultures of discipline, competence and success. These cultures, in turn, build grounded and consistently successful companies.

Courage – We have addressed courage at length, in one form or another, in our leadership chapter. At its simplest, courage is the wherewithal to make difficult but necessary decisions. It's the nerve to take risks, to make bets, to be willing to invest in new technologies, in new people, in new markets *before* other companies do. Courage also manifests itself in the ability to let go of the past: obsoleting products, business units and revenue streams. Some of the greatest acts of courage we have witnessed in recent years haven't involved big investments in AI and IoT, although those often do qualify as courageous plays, but rather, involved decisions by companies to disrupt themselves, to push off from familiar shores, to abandon the safety of tried and true (but fading) cash cows. Companies that disrupt themselves rather than wait to be disrupted exhibit that kind of courage. Companies that kill the business they were to become the business they need to be exhibit that kind of courage also.

When Apple decided to become a phone company rather than just a computer company, that was courage and it paid off. When IBM decided to transition from hardware to the Cloud, that was an act of courage also. When Amazon transitioned from being an online bookseller to become an online retailer, then a purveyor of content, then a first-mover in smart, voice-activated devices, these were all acts of courage as well. A company that can evolve, take chances, and jettison dead weight to repeatedly reinvent itself demonstrate the importance of courage in the larger futureproofing equation.

Conversely, companies that aren't founded on cultures of courage play it safe. They don't make risky investments in new technologies, skills or markets. They don't abandon old SKUs for fear of angering their most change-averse customers. They don't adopt new operational models or tread into unfamiliar territory. In business, the absence of courage isn't necessarily cowardice, but it is a void that, when left unfilled, keeps companies from seizing opportunities when they arise. Anyone who has ever run a company for any amount of time knows how precious and rare those kinds of opportunities are. Without the courage to seize them and capitalize on them, they are squandered. Sometimes, courage in business just comes down to knowing when to jump.

Authenticity – Before "authenticity" became a buzzword, it was the hallmark of every great brand, from Levi's and Ray Ban to Coca Cola and Harley Davidson. If your company isn't authentic, if your brand isn't authentic, if your product aren't authentic, then what are they? Inauthentic? Fake? Authenticity is the heart and soul of value. Authenticity is what makes a real Cartier watch worth more than a knockoff. Authenticity is what makes gelato different from just plain old ice cream. It's what makes experiences remarkable.

Authenticity is also the promise of truth in advertising, of quality manufacturing and of shared values. Authenticity is the promise that, when a CEO tells you something, you can believe it.
Great companies, companies that manage to repeatedly futureproof themselves, understand the value of authenticity. It *means* something to have that BMW logo on the hood of that car. It *means* something to have that "certified organic" stamp on the package. It *means* something that the label says "handmade by artisans" or "Made in the USA" or "established 1879." Authenticity means you're real. Companies that nurture cultures of authenticity tend to fare better than companies that don't focus on it or only pay lip service to it. Nothing kills the authenticity of a brand like a lie or dissonance between what that company claims and what the company actually does.

"An absolute commitment to quality" will be undone by a string of catastrophic failures and product recalls. "Handmade in the USA" will be undone by an undercover news report showing your products being made in sweatshops outside of the U.S. "The most powerful cybersecurity product on the planet" will be undone by massive data breaches that exploited flaws in your code.

Be known for what you deliver, not what you claim. Authenticity is your place on the value spectrum and your word. Companies that survive disruption know how to leverage that trait to remain credible, regardless of how much markets and tastes may change around them.
Reputation – Our discussion about authenticity has bled a bit into what we want to say about reputation, and that's okay. There's a good deal of overlap between some of these traits, and it's a good thing that you sometimes can't tell exactly where one ends and the next begins. Reputation, like authenticity, speaks to trust and expectations. Your reputation informs the market of what to expect, right? The best. The fastest. The most delicious. The most fun to use. The easiest UI. The most powerful. The safest. Also, it can be the worst, the slowest, the most poorly designed, the buggiest, the most dangerous (not in a good way), the ugliest, or the least reliable.

A company's reputation is a manifestation of its market effectiveness. It doesn't matter what the ads say. If your cars keep getting recalled, if your computers keep crashing, if your phones catch fire in your customers' pockets, if you falsified your own emissions test results, if your customer service is horrible, if you overbook your flights then violently remove passengers who don't want to surrender seats they feel they paid for, if you employ sweatshops to manufacture your products, if you discriminate against women and minorities, if you turn a blind eye to an internal culture of sexual harassment, if your conflict-free diamonds aren't really conflict free, if your security software quietly collects your customers' personal data and you then turn around and sell that data to third parties, if you keep getting caught using patents without their owner's permission, your company's reputation will suffer.

What does this have to do with futureproofing a company? Reputations also focus on innovation and adaptability. Who will Wall Street bet on during periods of disruption? Companies with a reputation for innovation and resiliency, or companies that have historically had trouble adapting to change? Same equation: Who will consumers bet on?

Which Cloud services company will fare better, the one with all the data breaches, or the one with all the big clients and zero major breaches to report? Which electric car company will fare better, the one with the proven track record of excellence or the one with inconsistent results? If reputation is important in periods of stability and consolidation, it is all the more important in periods of disruption and change. Because, when things become uncertain, people (investors, consumers, even employees) look for leaders and companies they can trust, with reputations for making the best out of uncertain times, and those that will get them through it all with as little drama and friction as possible.

One recent example of the importance of reputation to the lifecycle of a number of companies has nothing to do with technology at all, but rather focuses on cultural change. We were days from finishing this book when the "Alt-Right," a confederation of white nationalist organizations encompassing neo-Nazis, the KKK, and other supremacist groups, converged in Charlottesville, Virginia, to participate in a massive rally. Two law enforcement officers died in a helicopter crash while monitoring the rally from the air, and Heather Heyer, a counter demonstrator, was killed when an individual with alleged white supremacist ties drove his car into a crowd of people protesting Nazis and the Klan. Fast forward several days as the U.S. processed the violence and horror they witnessed in Charlottesville during that rally and the hatred on display online. Several companies decided to take action.

GoDaddy removed a leading neo-Nazi website, one with ties to the rally, from their service. Google followed suit, along with Twitter, Facebook, Spotify, Paypal, and Instagram.

Airbnb refused to rent properties to these same groups.

Cloudflare CEO Matthew Prince explained in televised interviews why his company also banned the website and emphasized the risk associated with that decision. The risk wasn't related to political fallout, death threats or anything of the sort, although those types of threats are certainly within the realm of possibilities. What Prince talked about was the danger of infrastructure companies in the internet "stack," as he referred to it, making editorial decisions as to what speech they want to allow and what speech they want to silence. The risk, in his mind, had nothing to do with being anti-Nazi or anti-racist or making a political statement, but in setting a precedent for censorship by companies with the power to control content and access to the internet. That too was a concern regarding his company's reputation. The credibility of his company and industry was at stake, and he made a strong argument for the industry to standardize clear rules of conduct, terms of service, due process, and transparency so that, when organizations and groups are sanctioned by companies like Cloudflare, they understand why, the public understands why and neither the industry nor the companies that make it up are harmed as a result.

Another dimension of this reputation management equation related to this ideologically toxic website's praise of Cloudflare and its suggestion that the company was allegedly friendly to its ideology and an ally to its cause. Here's a quick reputation management test. A Neo-Nazi website praises your company and characterizes it as an ally. What do you do? Most companies will immediately do whatever they can to distance themselves from that PR grenade. Even when companies try to stay out of politics, some situations require immediate, decisive and public action.

During the same week, we saw a number of major U.S. companies abandon presidential business advisory councils after the President of the United States responded somewhat poorly (and some might say ambiguously) to the problem of white supremacy and "Alt-Right" extremism in the U.S. The CEOs of Merck, Intel, 3M, Campbell Soup, Under Armour, and the Alliance for American Manufacturing resigned from their advisory council in response to the President's remarks. Apple's CEO pledged to donate $1 million each to the Anti-Defamation League and the Southern Poverty Law Center. For days, companies that previously remained as politically neutral as possible, as they tend to serve customers from all ideological and political backgrounds, saw themselves forced to distance themselves from an association they must have deemed dangerous to their companies' reputations.

There is a much larger discussion to be had about the role courage also plays into decisions like these. The nuances between the timing and specifics of each of these companies' individual courses of action are fascinating if you want to take the time to explore them. But, if we look at this milestone in recent history solely through the prism of reputation management, it is clear that reputation matters a lot. Companies that nurture their reputations, invest in them, protect them, and weigh the daily calculus of media optics against the long arc of history, tend to be better and faster at being tainted or harmed by crises. From denouncing hate groups and steering clear of unnecessary controversy to nurturing reputations built on leadership, innovation and courage, reputation management is a key component of futureproofing for organizations of all sizes.

HOW CULTURE ULTIMATELY BRINGS THE 7 PILLARS TOGETHER.

The key to understanding how culture brings the seven pillars of futureproofing together lies in understanding that culture is process.

Think about cultures of transparency, for instance. What makes a culture of transparency a culture of transparency? How does an organization build a culture of transparency? How does that work? First, you have to decide that transparency is important and it needs to be a fundamental trait of your organization. Then, you have to find ways of institutionalizing transparency across your organization, right? You define what transparency is. You articulate it. You explain why it matters. You create guidelines for how to achieve it. You establish systems of rewards and sanctions to ensure that everyone across the organization has skin in the game. You create a framework of transparency, best practices and accountability. That's process. It doesn't matter if the culture you are trying to create prioritizes transparency, innovation, amazing customer service, gorgeous industrial design, workforce diversity, fast delivery, authenticity, employee happiness, the coolest customer experiences, always the lowest prices, engineering genius, honesty, product durability, or worry-free banking. Culture is process.

When we study companies that tend to weather change well, or at least appear to be prepared to navigate change and disruption, what we find is that their cultures drive them toward prioritizing all seven of our pillars:

1. Experiences

2. People

3. Change

4. Innovation

5. Leadership and Transformation

6. Technology

7. Culture

In other words, futureproofed companies tend to enjoy cultures of experiences. From Disney to Starbucks, BMW to Tesla and Netflix to Apple, cultures of experience tend to win. There's a reason Google obsesses about how fast their searches are. There's a reason Coca Cola likes to insert the sound of one of their cans or bottles being cracked open in so many of their commercials. There's a reason ergonomics, packaging, software design, scent marketing, and a hundred more features of experience design are so important to companies that conquer markets and survive when others don't.

They also have people-focused cultures. Internally, these cultures are reflected by a focus on hiring, developing and retaining the best people, getting the most out of their people, turning employees into advocates, turning departments into teams, learning how to motivate them, train them, keep them engaged, and so on. They invest in people because, if they don't, if they choose to look at employees as "headcount," if they push them too hard, don't motivate them properly, make them feel underappreciated, they will become disengaged, and a disengaged workforce is an ineffective workforce. A disengaged workforce isn't going to be innovative, friendly or fun to work with. A disengaged workforce won't go the extra mile when it matters. A disengaged workforce won't collaborate very well, and it won't be particularly friendly to each other or customers. Companies that get this wrong, or don't prioritize this, create cultures of apathy, resentment, erosion, and even hostility. It's difficult to futureproof your organization when half of your employees don't really want to be there, and the other half don't want to all row the boat in the same direction.

Externally, people-focused cultures are characterized by an obsession with customers: Understanding them better, communicating with them better, engaging with them better, making them happy, making them trust you, making them love your products, and making them want to share experiences you created for them with family and friends. Look at any company that has endured over the years, and you will find that they have a deep internal focus on customers. Before the days of big and deep data analytics, they had to rely on instinct, relationships and market research, but the focus was always there. What now helps Amazon understand its customers better is just a digital version of what made all brick and mortar retailers successful before the age of the internet: Watching customers, talking with customers, studying how they shop, understanding price elasticity, measuring the effectiveness of coupons and special offers, testing different decors, different floor plans, moving things around, listening to complaints and suggestions, and studying what their customers liked about their competitors. Companies with cultures that focus on people tend to last. Companies that take people for granted, and whose cultures don't focus on people, tend to fade into obsolescence.

Companies that enjoy cultures of change obviously have an advantage over everyone else in times of disruption and transformation. They've already baked change into their DNA. Now, to be fair, most companies until perhaps two decades ago didn't focus on this on their own. They had to incorporate change into their cultures to survive. Many were on the brink, or may have felt that they were, and realized that building internal cultures of change was a question of short- and long-term survival. For many of these companies, this shift wasn't easy. They were dragged kicking and screaming into it. Some didn't quite manage to make those cultures stick, and they paid the price. Those that did avoided catastrophe and find themselves more prepared to keep adapting to disruption. McDonald's is an example of a company that has weathered change well and continues to. Does McDonald's face challenges at a time when people around the world are becoming more conscious of healthy lifestyles and the environmental impact of fast food restaurants? Yes. Does McDonald's face challenges from a growing ecosystem of fast, low-cost restaurant choices that hungry customers enjoy? Of course. Looking at how well McDonald's has adapted to change over time, we are confident that the fast food giant will adapt to these disruptions also.

Cultures of innovation tend to go hand-in-hand with cultures of change. Innovation is the catalyst of change, after all. Without it, change would happen much more slowly, if at all. One of the reason the Middle Ages lasted so long is that innovation wasn't really a focus. An absence of innovation creates stagnation. Consequently, periods of rapid innovation coincide with periods of rapid change, and companies with cultures of innovation understand the connection between innovation and change more intimately than most. Cultures of innovation always have to push the envelope faster and harder than everyone else. The technology and tools they use are always obsolete to tear past their previous boundaries. Take our earlier story of Hewlett-Packard building revolutionary audio oscillators for Disney, for instance. Disney needed to innovate. Disney partnered with Hewlett-Packard to get it done. The revolutionary experience this helped create revolutionized not only the movie business, but the movie theater business as well. The ripple effects of that innovation manifested themselves as change. Neither Disney nor Hewlett-Packard were the same companies they had been before that partnership. They both changed as a result. The same is true of every company, from Toyota and Dunkin Donuts to Samsung and GE.

The one critical advantage that cultures of innovation have over cultures of change is that a culture of innovation is almost always inherently a culture of change. Cultures of change are adaptable, agile and fluid, and can therefore react to stresses and reform themselves into more effective versions of themselves. However, cultures of innovation *drive* that change making them that much more effective. Cultures of innovation aren't just well equipped to survive disruption and make the most of it. They are the best equipped to drive that disruption. Cultures of innovation find themselves in the unique position of being able to disrupt entire industries. They are the apex predators of the innovation food chain, minus the food and predator parts, obviously. Look at companies like Google, Facebook, Amazon, Tesla, and Apple. Think about how they have radically transformed the world by way of focusing on innovation and continue to do so. Now think about the companies whose innovations feed into the Apples and Teslas and Amazons of the world. Companies like Qualcomm and Intel and Dassault Systemes, without whose IP portfolios and solutions, most of the innovation and amazing products we take for granted today would probably not exist. We have looked far and wide for futureproofed companies that don't have cultures of innovation, and we haven't found any. From Cartier and Burberry to General Mills and Cadillac, even brands that were popular before cordless phones were a thing have always been propped up by cultures of innovation.

Cultures of leadership are no different. You can almost set your watch to the cycles of growth and stagnation that companies experience when they take their cultures of leadership to heart and when they merely pay them lip service. Steve Jobs was the obvious example, but the same is true everywhere. Leaders lead. When "leaders" don't lead, who does? Virgin isn't peak Virgin without Richard Branson. Tesla isn't peak Tesla without Elon Musk. Facebook isn't peak Facebook without Mark Zuckerberg. Leaders grab the wheel and put their foot on the gas. When leaders go, and cultures of leadership turn into cultures of management, the foot comes off the gas and the car starts making a lot more stops to figure out where it should go next. This isn't all about superstar CEOs, by the way. True cultures of leadership have to transcend monolithic cults of personality so that every CEO that comes next is also a leader, not just a manager.

True cultures of leadership develop leaders at every level of the organization, from the most junior hire and the most underfunded project manager on up to the senior VPs and even the board of directors. There's a trick to spotting true cultures of leadership. They're the companies that do well regardless of who the CEO is. Pop quiz: Who is the CEO of Nestle? Who is the CEO of Harley Davidson? Who is the CEO of Nike? Who is the CEO of GE? Who is the CEO of Disney? If you know the answer to all of those questions, congratulations. Now can you list their predecessors? If yes, we're *very* impressed. If you can't, that's okay. We're just trying to make a point. True cultures of leadership don't slow down, deflate or implode when their superstar CEOs move on. They just keep going, improving and growing.

When organizations put technology at the center of their cultures, it's probably a safe bet that they're going to be sensitive to change and adaptation. The thing about technology is that it is always depreciating, falling behind and growing a little more obsolete by the day. Technology-centric cultures tend not to let their tech grow too dusty or moldy. They are always looking for ways of improving the technology they have, getting more out of it or replacing it with something better. If you're a retailer, payment systems are a core technology, right? A technocentric retailer is going to update its checkout technology often. A retailer that has somehow managed to not build a technocentric culture isn't. In an experience-driven economy, that isn't a mere detail. If your technology is outdated and burdensome, your checkout experience might take too long and cart abandonment increases. This is true on the web and in brick-and-mortar stores. Conversely, if your checkout technology is on the cutting edge, not only do you turn the checkout experience into an unexpected delight, you also add another gold star to your overall brand story. Your company isn't a laggard. It's making smart decisions. It's aware of the subtle ways in which the world is changing. If it's getting this right, it's probably getting a lot of other things right too. Think about the impact this can have in consumer confidence.

Technology-centric cultures are especially well-equipped to do well now that so much technology is interwoven with the world around us. From the machines that always deliver the exact same coffee experience no matter what Starbucks you go to and collision-avoidance systems in your next car, to the hybrid cloud ecosystem and IoT-based services model that will drive the next healthcare revolution, technology is the engine of progress, change, transformation, and disruption. This is nothing new. Steam technology transformed travel and manufacturing. The telegraph, radio, printing press, X-ray machine, automobile, jet engine, forge, spear, transistor, and panini oven—technology is always at the heart of market success in one way or another. Technology-centric cultures tend to be futureproof. Companies whose cultures fail to understand the value technology or treat it as an afterthought tend to come and go, but mostly go.

Lastly, we come to culture. There is obviously no such thing as a culture of culture. There are, however, organizations that understand the value of culture, the function of culture, and, therefore, the power of culture. The most successful among them also realize that culture is a process, and those are the companies that are able to create the most consistent experiences, internally and externally. In the best case scenario, these are positive experiences. In many cases, where organizations either deliberately or negligently create toxic cultures, those experiences tend to be negative. Great cultures can, on occasion, sprout out of nowhere on their own, but if there is nothing there to feed them, to nurture them, to make sure they grow strong roots. Culture isn't something organizations can afford to leave to change, and so cultures that understand the value of culture tend to create self-fulfilling mechanisms of positive culture-building that ultimately play a role in the futureproofing process.

HOW HAVE MAJOR BRANDS AND HIGH-PER-FORMING COMPANIES REAPED THE REWARDS OF NURTURING STRONG, UNIQUE CULTURES?

We have room for one last example, and since we're on the subject of culture, let's make this one about beer.

Samuel Adams was founded in 1984 by Jim Koch, a Harvard alumnus who tried his hand at finance and consulting before realizing that what he really wanted to do was make beer.

Let's pause right here to appreciate that Samuel Adams was, like many futureproof companies, a passion project. Koch wasn't just going through the motions of starting a company he thought could be successful. He loved beer. He was passionate about beer. He built a beer company that was always going to be different from the rest. Whatever Samuel Adams' culture is today is the culmination of that original spark and it owes much of its years of success to it.

Anyway, legend has it that Koch perfected his Boston Lager recipe in his kitchen, then went around from bar to bar selling it (in what must have been limited batches). Although we take today's micro-brew ecosystem for granted, remember that back in the early 1980s, there were only about a hundred microbreweries around the U.S. "Big Beer" (Miller, Coors and Budweiser) dominated the market. His lager was a success, though, so he moved production from his kitchen to the former Haffenreffer Beer brewery in 1985, where things started to scale.

Fastforward to 2015 and 2016. Samuel Adams (or rather the Boston Beer Company) is now a $900 million per year business that produces four million barrels of craft beer per year. The problem is that the revolution it started back in 1984 was a little too successful. The U.S. now has more than 4,000 breweries pushing out craft beers. Three new beer companies set up shop each day. And so Koch's company now finds itself struggling to retain its market share against the thousands of exciting craft beer choices available to consumers. How do you overcome this challenge? Well, if you're a passionate CEO who loves what he does, and has built an agile, adaptable and innovative company, you do this:

- Hire great people who are just as passionate about your business as you are and give them all the responsibility they care to handle. Train them. Develop them. Give them the tools to experiment, express themselves professionally, and grow. If they love working there, they will put love into their work and, at a company driven by passion, that means everything.

- Hire dotcom refugees early and see if they can inject your organization with new ideas. Not as IT professionals, but as beermakers. Crosstrain them. Develop them. Make them more than just tech-savvy employees with a narrow lane of expertise.

- Jennifer Glanville, brewery manager at Samuel Adams in Boston, was a tech professional when she joined the company in the early 2000s. She knew next to nothing about brewing beer, but she learned and, over time, was given license to experiment and play with crazy ideas, which paid off. For instance, she created the first pumpkin beer for Halloween, before every other beer brand caught on and started making their own. She also launched a Nano-Brewery project as Sam Adams, which now basically serves as an in-house prototyping lab for beer innovation. Half of her staff is made up of women, which probably helps inject more variety into the beers that her team comes up with than if most of her staff were men. You get the idea: Passion + curiosity + tech = innovation + opportunity + adaptability.

• Create a culture of open collaboration. There are no silos at Samuel Adams. The company's brewers all help each other practice the basics, develop new beers, perfect new techniques, and experiment every single day. They are constantly measuring, making incremental improvements, testing ideas, challenging each other, helping each other solve problems, and so on.

As a result, Samuel Adams remains the No. 1 craft beermaker in the United States, even in the middle of a veritable tsunami of disruption from thousands of small, local, hyper-authentic competitors. How? By creating a business culture that continuously innovates, delights and remains true to its passion for authenticity, quality and relevance.

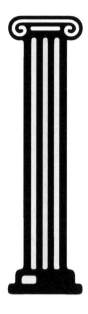

CONCLUSION:

When we set out to write this book we hoped to accomplish two things:

1. Help our readers better understand the shared traits and methodologies of companies that already have cracked the code of successful digital transformations.

2. Provide readers of our previous book, *Building Dragons*, with useful lessons and case studies from the trenches of digital transformation that they can apply to their own business endeavors.

After reviewing nearly 200 case studies and engaging with change leaders at some of the world's great brands, we discovered that the difference between companies that manage digital transformation well and those that struggle with change in general comes down to only seven cardinal elements. Part trait, part focal point, part operational building block, these seven foundational elements acted as what seemed to us like the pillars of a sort of future-proofing mechanism. The more companies and digital transformation programs we looked at, the more a pattern emerged. This pattern informed the structure of this book and its title.

It isn't to say that these seven pillars alone are what separate futureproof companies from the rest of the field. Dozens of additional qualities, some of them shared, some of them truly unique, also lend themselves to the ability that some companies have to adapt to change better than others and set themselves apart. Those unique differences can be found in almost every company, and that is good news. What isn't always there, though, is a focus on the seven big ones. And, by focus, we mean an *awareness* of these seven pillars, a clear *understanding* of just how critical they are to the success of every business, and a *decision* from business leaders to invest their time, money and energy into them to be able to tackle the long road ahead. These seven pillars are in the DNA of all the companies that pulled away from the pack and continue to inspire consumers and investors around the world, no matter how fast things change around them.

Experiences: Why people fall in love with brands and stay in love.

People: The heart and soul of every organization.

Change: What we fear the most for all the wrong reasons.

Leadership and transformation: The two always go hand-in-hand.

Innovation: The genius at the core of every successful business.

Technology: The tools that give us control and power over change.

Culture: What gives companies their traits and personalities.

It's important to note that, while every company we discussed in this book focuses in some way on all seven of these pillars, we also found that none of these companies excel equally at making the most of all seven. For instance, Amazon has built its success on experiences and innovation, but has struggled with culture, as high performance expectations and stress on employees have crept into the equation. For its part, Qualcomm has built a strong culture and has led market innovation around the world, but has struggled to make connections down market with consumers, most of whom unknowingly use their inventions every day. There is no perfect company. No organization gets all seven pillars 100 percent right, and that's okay. There's always room for improvement. If there weren't, business wouldn't be all that fun.

A useful exercise at this juncture is for you to make a short list of companies you love and admire, a short list of companies you dislike, and grade them all against the seven future-proofing pillars. It could be any company: Apple, Tesla, McDonald's, Uber, Wells Fargo, United Airlines, Netflix, Zappos, Ford, your favorite local coffee shop, your least favorite grocery store... make those two lists as long as you want. Gauge which of the seven pillars they obviously focus on and which of the seven pillars they don't. Grade them. Do they get an A? Do they get an F? Do they fall somewhere in between? Now look at their scores and see how high grades give some companies a significant market advantage and low grades make other companies vulnerable. Look for companies that score fairly well across all seven pillars and think about how much better equipped they are to weather change than companies that don't.

Don't just stop there. Also consider which of these pillars companies that score consistently well across all seven can afford to get a B- in, for instance, instead of an A. Gauge the importance of these pillars relative to each other. If these companies can only afford to score an A in three of them, which ones should they be? Which ones does it make sense to prioritize? Does it appear that these companies have already made that calculation? What does that say about their awareness and strategic choices?

Equipped with these insights, now perform the same quick analysis of your own company. What do you see? Ideally, you were already focusing on all seven without realizing it. If so, which ones are your company prioritizing? Knowing what you now know, what changes and improvements do you plan to make in the next six months? Once you realize that the seven pillars are all important, but not necessarily *equally* important to your business, you can use that insight to determine where investments of time, money and energy should be focused to accelerate your transformation.

Less ideally but perhaps more realistically, you now realize that your company was already focusing on several of the pillars, but not all of them. If that's the case, you now have a roadmap to help you fill the gaps in your future-proofing strategy. As we've seen, some of the world's biggest and most enduring brands only recently started focusing on all seven pillars. You may not have fallen as far behind as you might think. There's still time to catch up.

If you are a small business or a startup owner, it's easy to get caught up in the mystique of unicorns. There are several pretty amazing tales of wild success there. There's no doubt about it, when it works, it works. But when you read about Bill Hewlett (HP) or Howard Schultz (Starbucks) and how they built their companies, what you find is that they were always much more dragon than unicorn. Right from the start. It was years of hard work and a relentless pursuit of their goals that led them to becoming the great enterprises they are today. Even Reed Hastings of Netflix worked tirelessly for well over a decade before Netflix became the global phenomenon that it is today. Time after time, company after company, continued success and growth were driven by fast experimentation, courageous leadership, a focus on the right things, and great stories that touch all seven of the pillars we outline in this book.

If, on the other hand, you are leading an already established enterprise (or you are somewhere on your way to leading part of one), you may find yourself looking over your shoulder, hoping for the best but preparing for the worst. You may be reading headlines about disruption and Fortune 500 overhauls and wondering if your company will be the next tragic victim of disruption, like Blockbuster, Kodak, and Xerox, companies that were giants in their heyday and are all but ashes and dust today. The good news is that you don't have to end up like they did. You have a roadmap now, a framework. You know where to begin, if that's where your company is, and you know what to focus on next if you were already on your way. You understand how a positive shift in culture, methods, capabilities, and strategic focus will lead to better business results, which is why you set out to digitally transform in the first place.

Regardless of what kind of business you lead, or how far along that business is today, whether you are big, small or somewhere in between, change is the only constant. It's inevitable. You're either going to control it or be controlled by it. Companies that win choose to control it. It's that simple. As leaders, we all make that choice every day. We either decide to lead or to not. We decide to build and lead teams and businesses and prepare them for what lies ahead or to sit back and not do that. That's the essence of leadership, isn't it? Making that choice? When you push everything else aside—the titles, compensation, authority, and power—effective leadership in today's business world can be distilled down to this—you are either building dragons or you aren't. There's no in between.

Brand graveyards are filled with incumbent brands that believe their own myths of longevity and invincibility, right? Well, leadership graveyards are filled with the career graves of incumbent executives who focused on the wrong things and fell asleep at the wheel.

The fact that you picked up this book and read it shows a measure of initiative that few people have. It's a leadership trait that already sets you apart from the crowd. And, in a world where far too many people spend inordinate amounts of time resisting change and improvement, those among us who see the value in it and are equipped to help drive it are invaluable to the world of business. It's a tremendously marketable skill, especially with what's coming. We hope that you have found this book insightful and helpful, and that you will now be able to share what you've learned with as many decision makers and business leaders as you can, whether they are part of your organization or not. More importantly, we hope that you will apply many of the insights we have shared with you here to your own business and make it truly futureproof.

ABOUT THE AUTHORS

DANIEL NEWMAN

Daniel Newman is the Principal Analyst of Futurum Research and the CEO of Broadsuite Media Group. Living his life at the intersection of people and technology, Daniel works with the world's largest technology brands exploring Digital Transformation and how it is influencing the enterprise.

From Big Data to IoT to Cloud Computing, Newman makes the connections between business, people and tech that are required for companies to benefit most from their technology projects, which leads to his ideas regularly being cited in CIO.Com, CIO Review and hundreds of other sites across the world. A 5x Best Selling Author including his most recent "Building Dragons: Digital Transformation in the Experience Economy," Daniel is also a Forbes, Entrepreneur and Huffington Post Contributor. MBA and Graduate Adjunct Professor, Daniel Newman is a Chicago Native and his speaking takes him around the world each year as he shares his vision of the role technology will play in our future.

OLIVIER BLANCHARD

Olivier Blanchard is a Senior Analyst with Futurum Research, where he focuses on the global impact of technology disruption, best practices in digital transformation and change management, and the future of business.

Olivier is also the best-selling author of Social Media ROI: Managing and Measuring Social Media Efforts in Your Organization, and the co-author of 'Building Dragons: Digital Transformation in the Experience Economy', 'The Ultimate Field Guide to Digital Program Management', and 'Futureproof: 7 Key Pillars for Digital Transformation Success.' In addition to his work as an analyst and writer, Olivier is also a sought-after keynote speaker, subject-matter expert, and industry thought leader.

ACKNOWLEDGMENTS

A lot of people helped make this book possible, and we would be remiss if we didn't thank them for their invaluable contributions to this process. In no particular order:

Endless gratitude to Shelly Kramer, Eric Vidal, Brian Fanzo, Herns Pierre-Jerome, Pete Lancia, Joe Schuman, Jens Meggers, Shelley Newark, Vincent Brissot, Diane Eli Grotte, Sarah Moore, Patrick Moorhead, Jim Hunt, Jeremiah Owyang, Michele Null, Scott Monty, Angela Lipscomb, Kristin Wehmeyer, Augie Ray, Francois Gossieaux, Josh Bernoff, Linsey Dyson, Ursula Ringham, Emily Mui, Ginger Shimp, Alan Berkson, Kristi Colvin, Becca Taylor, Rebecca Wissinger, Roby Di Giovine, Monica Menghini, Lluis Altes, Shannon Peng, and Rani Mani for the amazing conversations, insights and ideas that helped steer us in the right direction. Huge thanks to Kenna Griffin, our fearless editor and expert word wrangler, for cleaning up our manuscript, and to Kristi Colvin, April Butten, and Sebastian Melchor for making the book look a lot prettier than we could have ever hoped.

We also want to send a special shoutout to the amazing students in Daniel's Graduate Topics Course in Digital Transformation at North Central College who helped us with some of our background research, and particularly Richard Zirngibl, whose work provided background for our insights into Nike.